MW01257414

Bee Native! Flower Power
An Easy Guide to Choosing Native Flowers for your
Garden to Help Pollinators.

Midwest Edition

Written and Illustrated by Flora C. Caputo

Author and Owner of *The Urban Domestic Diva,*
a food & lifestyle blog and social
space for sharing the love of food, gardening, crafting
and simply making the world lovelier, one pixel at a time.

ISBN: 9781099534911
1st edition, 3rd printing 2021

***

*Dedicated to my Nonno Esposito, who was always
growing something in some dirt, no matter where he was.*

*And to my husband Rich, who never bats an eye
when I tell him about my next crazy idea or endeavor.
You always have my back, luv.
Thank you.*

***

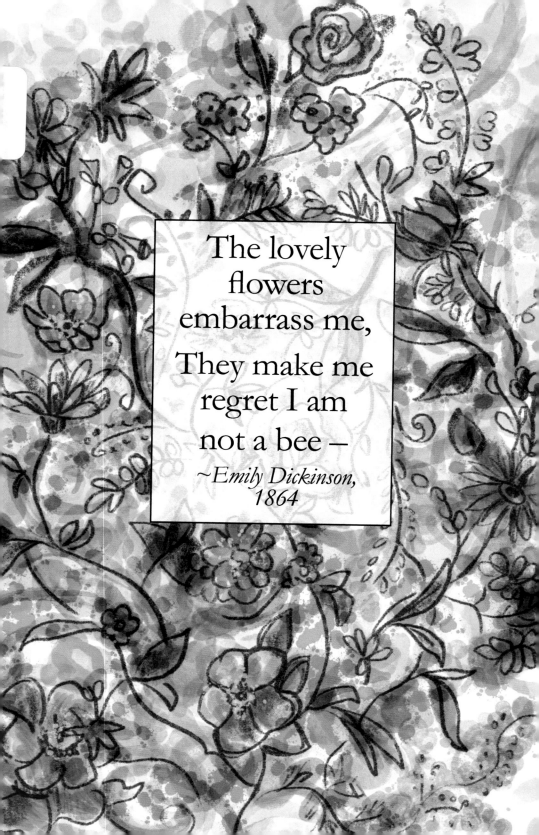

The lovely flowers embarrass me, They make me regret I am not a bee –

~Emily Dickinson, 1864

Table of Contents:

Introduction:

A love of growing things.

I began my journey into gardening when I had an apartment with my first balcony. The view was horrible, overlooking an alley and a dingy yard that my landlord cared little about. But with a handful of window boxes and pots, I transformed my little outdoor space. into an oasis filled with annuals, vines, and edible herbs. My mother always tried to get me to do yard work growing up, and I fought it tooth and nail. Because it wasn't my yard or my plants. There is a greater sense of responsibility, love, and care for the living things you plant when you are the one that put them there. I am not sure when the change happened. But she is pretty surprised at my love of gardening now. It really started with my grandfather, who sowed some gardening love in me early. He knew in his heart the seeds would take root and grow when the time was right, even if he wasn't going to be around to see them grow.

My grandfather would take me up to his rooftop garden when I was very little. Herbs and tomatoes as far as the eye could see were growing in rusted out coffee and tomato cans. All summer long he provided fresh tomatoes and herbs to my Nonna for the revered Sunday sauce. My grandparents (as well as my parents) were Italian and didn't speak a word of English. My grandfather missed his garden in Naples, Italy. He was trying to grow a little piece of it on that grey, noisy, city rooftop on Taylor Street in Chicago, plant by plant. I loved going up there to check on the plants and help him shoo away the pigeons. I felt like I was on top of the world, and this is really where my love for growing things started.

Fast forward through three houses, many garden overhauls, and one poison ivy incident, and my gardening know-how has grown. I've killed many things and I've grown many things. As a younger gardener, I loved all the cultivars the garden catalogs featured between their shiny, colorful pages. I fell in love with the English roses, peonies, hybrid irises and the like. In fact, I still love them. But as I've gotten older, I've gotten wiser. Not all cultivars work long-term in your garden. Experiments can get costly and somewhat depressing. As I learned my lessons through the years, various friends gifted me native wildflowers and plants. I noticed, season after season, that while some of my expensive cultivars looked good for a time, they would eventually die off. These hybrids didn't tolerate large weather swings typical of the Midwest. But the natives thrived year after year with very little care or concern. I slowly began to plant more native perennials, and soon noticed an explosion of bees and butterflies visiting my yard.

As the news continued to be ominous about the lifespan of our pollinators, and the environment, the more natives I planted. I saw with my own eyes the proliferation of bees, butterflies, and birds in my little city garden. If I could make such an impact with small changes in a small space, imagine if more people did the same? How big of an impact could we all make together?

I discovered some challenges once I decided to focus on native plants. First, finding the right information around native plants and clarity around which ones were right for my garden was labor-intensive. Books about natives are giant tomes, organized alphabetically, with more information than one could ever need or want. I spent weekends pouring over books and websites with papers strewn all over my kitchen, filled with sketches of my garden beds. I dedicated hours and hours to this task every spring that I didn't have. I couldn't find easy resources focused on natives organized in a way people plan their garden.

When a book organizes plants alphabetically, you need to know what you're looking for already. If you plan as I do, you look at the height that you need for the space that you are planning for. Then you take into account sun needs. From there you fine-tune your plant choices based on your soil needs and finally, color. Turning my own frustration into purpose, I decided that there needed to be a book organized in this way. I hope this book brings ease to adding native plants to our gardens. I love cultivars and hybrids as much as any gardener. My two favorite plants in my garden are two English roses. I am not suggesting that you go "full-on native". But adding the right natives in the right spots can add long-lasting color to your yard. They will also provide long-lasting food and shelter for your local pollinators. You'll see more wildlife and activity in your yard, signaling that you are making a big impact. It's a win-win.

The second challenge is actually *finding* native plants to put in your yard. Native plants have fallen so out of favor over the years that many are rare or endangered, especially woodland natives. If certain natives don't produce a lot of seeds or take a long time to germinate and proliferate, they become harder to source. Many nurseries focus on hybrids and cultivars versus natives. After all, it's what sells. Although, I am seeing a swing back to the other direction. The more customers ask for natives, the greater the chance the nurseries see the trend and start selling natives again. To help with this, I've put native resources in the back of the book. There are many online sites that provide seeds and starter plants. There are a growing number of nurseries within your state that may sell native plants, too. But a word of caution here. In trying to get more natives in your yard please be were respectful of the wild. Many imperiled plants are in danger from gardeners and collectors such as ourselves. Many go to the wild and dig up natives and try to transplant them onto their own property. Plants that are tough to grow from seed, woodland wildflowers, plants from specialized habitats and plants that create few seeds are often the most vulnerable. In our effort to help our own ecosystem let's not hurt it by digging up plants from the wild. Also, buy from nurseries that propagate the plants they sell in a sustainable way. Be sure to do research and ask questions. Local forest preserves are now selling native plants at very affordable prices. I've tried to list as many as I could in the back of the book. Your local community and farmer's markets may be a treasure trove of native plant options for you as well. In time there will be such a demand for native plants that it will get easier to buy these gems for our gardens.

The Pollinator Problem

The biggest moments in history were actually caused by the smallest most imperceptible thing. Like a pebble in a pond, where that pebble dropped in the water ripples out, causing a big wave onto the shore. This analogy describes the issue of the world's pollinators. Our pollinators are small and sometimes you don't even notice that they're there. But their impact on our environment and the food supply chain is huge. That's why the pollinator problem is a very big problem. To put it in perspective, one out of three bites of our food comes to us thanks to a pollinator[1]. Food won't grow without pollination. Plants and flowers won't grow without pollination. Without plants, we won't have air. Without plants, we won't have food for much of our wildlife. From there the whole food chain deteriorates, and so does the environment. I'm not here to argue about the reality of global warming and who or what is to blame. The book is not about that. Facts are facts, and numbers of pollinators-and particularly bee populations, are in steep decline worldwide. Multifaceted causes are to blame.

In fact, global warming or climate change is a small piece of the puzzle when it comes to the decline. Other factors include agricultural stresses, aggressive mining, and simply trying to keep up with population growth. As more land gets covered in city cement or green lawns, more natural habitat is being taken away from pollinators. Over 150 million acres of farmland in the United States alone have been lost to urban sprawl[2]. Our love of green lawns means we are creating miles of green wastelands. Sure they're great for your kids to run on and look nice and neat. Full disclosure, I have a lawn, too! But lawns offer no nutritional value, shelter or nesting areas for pollinators or local wildlife. Add to our love of lawns our love of non-native species of plants for our gardens to the problem. Cultivars of peonies, delphinium, and azaleas offer beauty but have less nutritional value to give our pollinators. The introduction of non-native, invasive species of plants into our environment is also a problem. The plants tend to be very aggressive and compete for space, water, and sun, forcing out our native plants. Pesticide use is also a culprit. From keeping our lawns green to keeping our farm crops growing, pesticides use is prevalent. It can cause "colony collapse disorder" where full bee colonies die off. A friend of ours, who is an avid beekeeper in a near suburb of Chicago, experienced total bee colony collapse one year. Upset and baffled, he soon made the correlation between a recent neighborhood spraying of lawn service chemicals to his bees dying. The threat of pesticide is real and we need to address it. The last piece of the puzzle is

1 Pollinators in Trouble Worldwide, Living on Earth, https://www.loe.org/shows/segments.html?program-ID=16-P13-00010&segmentID=4, May 20, 2019
2 Why Native Plants Matter, National Audubon Society, https://www.audubon.org/content/why-native-plants-matter, May 20, 2019

climate change. Changes in weather and migration patterns are affecting the ecosystem. This affects bees, butterflies, birds and the plant life that supports them all.

The Native Plant Solution

So that's all the bad news. But don't feel overwhelmed. Here's the good news. Native plants are a quick and easy way to help the pollinators. In the course of the evolution of our planet, native plants and bees evolved in tandem. So the symbiotic relationship between the two is very natural. Mother Nature specially designed many flowers to accommodate and guide pollinators. It's actually quite fascinating and magical. From the way the stamens are grown on a flower to where the colors and designs are on petals to how tall the plant is in its natural habitat, natives have evolved to help their pollinators. In return, the plants give their helpers nectar, food and shelter. Both live on this earth to naturally help each other out.

Natives provide other benefits, too, as it relates to their greater ecological impact. They last longer than hybrids because they come from the local area. They can tolerate local weather swings because they've evolved within that location. Natives have long bloom times. They are often drought tolerant because of deep tap roots or a natural affinity to the area. Many natives have also learned to self propagate. Because of all this, gardeners need fewer chemicals to grow and care for natives. Across the board, native plants need fewer resources because they've adapted to their local soil and climate. When you use fewer resources than there is less stress on the environment. And let's not forget less stress on the gardener, who doesn't need to put as much work into caring for natives. Less work and more joy in the garden has always been my goal. Natives can help us all achieve it. So let's get started.

Let's Go.

My goal for this book was to inspire and help others make a big impact quickly and easily in their own yards. To that end, I kept this book very focused on favorite flowering native plants, flowering vines, and flowering ground cover. I didn't include every single native flowering plant. The list is very extensive. If you want more information because I've piqued your interest, there's plenty out there written by botanists and scientists. In the effort of ease and approachability, I kept the book very simple and focused. I did not include native trees, bushes, ferns or grasses. One, because those plants don't make as quick of an impact on local pollinators as the flowering wildflowers and woodland natives do. Two, because shrubs, bushes, and trees add a level of complexity, planning, commitment, investment, and labor. Putting in a tree takes more time and money. If I were planning on putting a tree in my yard, I would need alignment with my husband, first. Then I would need a plan on delivery and planting it. Native flowers are very easy to pop in the garden, no husband alignment required! I hope within one growing season, you can make some quick changes within your yard to help pollinators and with very little investment.

As you approach your garden planning while using my guide, it's important to understand your garden and design goals. Ask yourself what area are you working with? How much sun does it get? Is the soil very wet or very dry? Understanding your area is your first step before planning and planting natives. When I plan, I put tall, large plants towards the back of my garden beds or in corners. Then I stair step the plants as I move towards the front by placing medium plants in the middle. Then plant lower level or ground cover plants toward the front. But it depends on the space and what I'm trying to achieve.

Planning is easy. I hope that this book makes it even easier for you. I left you an area in the back of the book for notetaking. I want this book dirty, scruffy, full of notes and well-loved. Make a positive impact on your local pollinator population-and the environment as a whole, with some simple, small steps.

Consider the Bees:

To make it easier on our busy bees, consider the following when planning your garden:

-Plant plants in groups for easier foraging so the bees don't get tired hopping from plant to plant.

-Try to have something always in bloom, from early spring to late fall. Pollinators will have nectar throughout the season.

-Try to avoid pesticides or chemicals in your yard. Try using more natural products or create natural DIY solutions. For instance, Epsom salt is a natural way to green-up your lawn and strengthen plant roots instead of fertilizer. There are many homegrown remedies for the garden that work as well as store-bought chemicals.

-Provide shallow troughs or small bowls of water for bees. They need bee baths like birds need birdbaths.

-Keep areas of undisturbed ground around your yard, allowing for nesting sites. Most pollinating bees nest in the ground or in hollowed out stems and tree branches.

HONEY BEE 1.Worker. 2.Male. 3.Queen. 4 .5.COMMON HUMBLE BEE. LAPIDARY BEE. 6.Male. 7.Female. 8.MOSS or CARDER BEE. 9 DONOVAN'S HUMBLE BEE. 10.HARRIS' HUMBLE BEE. FALSE HUMBLE BEES. 11Apathus Vestalis. 12Apathus Rupestris.

Blackie & Son Glasgow, Edinburgh & London.

Consider the Butterflies:

As much as I tried to focus on bees, butterflies kept flitting into my research. You will find them mentioned throughout this book. Their numbers are diminishing as well. Consider the following in your planning to help out your local butterflies:

-Include nectar-producing native flowers in your mix of native plants

-Make sure you have native plants for early spring season and late fall season. It's those times of the year when butterflies are struggling for food. This is because most blooms either haven't started yet or have finished their lifecycle.

-Butterflies need shelter from the rain and some do over winter. So they like to use natural areas like shrubs or thick grasses for protection. Also, don't be so quick to clean up the debris and leaves from the fall. Butterflies that overwinter use those leaves and leaf litter for warmth and shelter.

-When picking native plants, consider host plants for butterflies. These are plants that provide a safe place for butterflies to lay eggs, and feed the caterpillars once they hatch. Butterflies can be "deadbeat parents". We can help by making sure we have host plants for our local baby butterflies.

Consider the Cold Zones:

The following illustration is based on the most recent map of the USDA in 2012. In my personal opinion, I think this map is too old, and I am not alone in this[3]. With climate change, my gardening instincts tell me that the zones are moving. I would also add, climate change is making weather prediction quite difficult. It doesn't take a scientist to know that the weather forecast changes drastically within 24 hours. Not a minor change, but a drastic 15-degree mistake-sometimes with an accumulation of snow or hail, or drought. So what can gardeners do?

My humble advice is this; use this zone map as a guide, but trust your instincts and your senses. Get to know your area, and get a read on what works for you and your neighbors. Also, as I mentioned in my introduction, if any plant species can tolerate the unpredictability of an area, it's a native plant. So trust your local flora and fauna. Observe what is working and living in your local gardens and yards. Watch what comes up early, or is staying evergreen in the winter. I am noticing quite a lot of my tender perennials staying green in the winter when mulched, even while contending with polar vortexes and record spring snows. That may be a sign that I can try more tender plants that prefer a slightly warmer zone. The rules of gardening always apply: use cold zones as a map, trust your gut, use your 5 senses and absorb your environment. Let it all guide your choices.

My poor magnolia tree suffered during a record-breaking snowstorm in mid-April, 2019. The accumulation in my yard was 6".

3 Matt Sauk, Gardener's Path, USDA PLANT HARDINESS ZONES HAVE CHANGED: WHAT YOU NEED TO KNOW, https://gardenerspath.com/how-to/hacks/hardiness-zone-changes/, May 22,2019

If you wish to read up on how climate change is affecting cold zones, here are a few links:
https://gardenerspath.com/how-to/hacks/hardiness-zone-changes/
https://www.arborday.org/media/mapchanges.cfm

12 http://www.news-gazette.com/living/2018-12-22/the-garden-climate-change-and-planting-part-i.html

USDA COLD ZONE MAP 2012

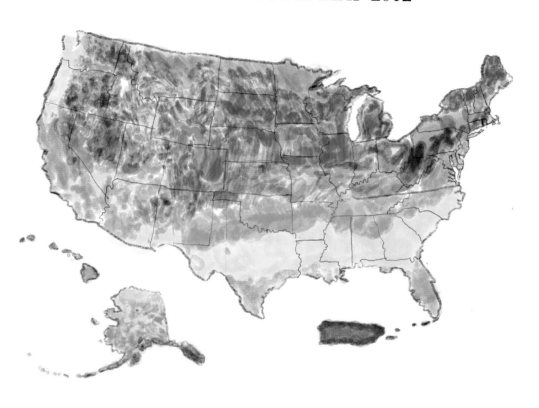

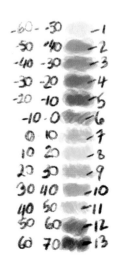

-60	-50	-1
-50	-40	-2
-40	-30	-3
-30	-20	-4
-20	-10	-5
-10	0	-6
0	10	-7
10	20	-8
20	30	-9
30	40	-10
40	50	-11
50	60	-12
60	70	-13

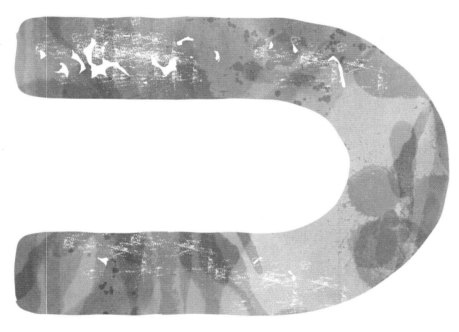
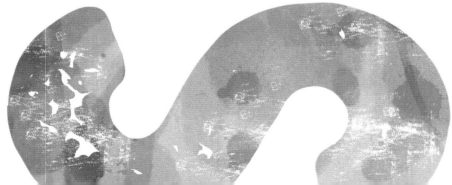

14

Full Sun
Native Flowers
6+ hours of sun

pasqueflower

Anemone patens

aka: prairie smoke, windflower

OVERVIEW

This is a neat flower. It's a unique prairie plant that gets its name from its fuzzy plumes once the flower has gone to seed. The plumes carry the plant's seeds and look like soft smoke thus its name. This plant blooms often in the old matted grass, leaves and various detritus of the previous fall. Its early bloom time makes it a harbinger of spring. The flowers range in color from white to a pastel lavender-blue, with starry yellow-gold centers. The solitary flowers are about 2"-3" in diameter, grounded by fern-like, densely hairy leaves.

GROWING NOTES

This flower does best in full sun but can tolerate light shade. Because of its ability to grow in last years old, dead leaves it actually thrives on neglect. So if you have a brown thumb, this may be the pant for you! It likes well-drained sandy or loamy soil and can tolerate dry conditions. Propagation is best by seeds but may take years for those plants to bear flowers. It is a very easy plant to divide and transplant by root division.

Zone 1-7

Blooms: early spring

Native Regions

crossvine

Bignonia capreolata

OVERVIEW

This is another one of my favorite flowering vines. It earned a spot in this book because it's well visited by many pollinators because of its sweet nectar. This sought after nectar is created by showy, bright orange blooms with deep red centers. Sometimes flowers are completely deep red. The 2½" tubular flowers look like bells climbing along the vines. The vines are semi-evergreen and feature glossy, tooth-edged oblong 4"-6" leaves. This native can be trained to grow on gates, fences, and trellises. It's called crossvine because the shape of a cross appears in the flesh of the stem when cut. This is an early nectar source for many pollinators, specifically hummingbirds. You'll notice that many manufactured hummingbird feeders mimic this red vine flower.

GROWING NOTES

Crossvine prefers well-drained, moist soil but isn't fussy and is a flexible grower. It can even thrive in clay or sandy soils. It can also tolerate part shade but will produce fewer blooms. Mulching plants in colder zones is prudent for the winter. Propagation is best by seeds, stem cuttings or root division.

Zone 5-9

Bloom time: mid spring-late summer

BUTTERFLY FAVORITE

BEE FAVORITE

Native Regions

19

Eastern trout lily

Erythronium americanum

aka: dogtooth violet, yellow adder's tongue, fawn lily

OVERVIEW

This is a very unique woodland plant with very interesting markings, making it look like it came from the Paleolithic era. It's an early spring wildflower, and the flowers are only visible for one month out of the year. Called a trout lily, on account of the speckled pattern on its leaves that look like trout fish. The leaves are 3" to 6" long and the flower stalks are 3" to 8" long. Each stalk bears one bright yellow flower, shaped like a lily, with three petals and three sepals and six brown stamens. These bright bursts of sunshine is a welcome sight for pollinators in early spring looking for food. Usually, in early spring, forests are still waking from dead leaves and debris.

GROWING NOTES

Being a woodland wildflower, the bulbs like moisture. It also needs cold treatment to resume the growth cycle in the spring. It's very versatile to any soil condition. Propagation as best by bulbs, root expansion or seeds. Seeds do take a long time to germinate and get established. So transplanting bulb offsets is the best way to propagate this very unique plant.

Zone 4-7

Bloom time: early-mid spring

Native Regions

21

FULL SUN

bluets

Houstonia caerulea

aka: quaker ladies, innocence, little bluets

OVERVIEW

These small, star-shaped petal flowers are usually seen in light blue to lilac to yellow. Each has a yellow center, and sit atop thin stems that have pairs of narrow tiny leaves all along their length. The best way to describe these tiny, pastel wonders is "perky". Leaves at the base of the plants are more numerous and ground the plant visually. The flowers themselves require cross-pollination for seeds, making it a very attractive plant for pollinators.

GROWING NOTES

This plant is exceptional for rock gardens and likes slightly acidic soil. Rocky areas can get droughty, and this plant does like moisture. Propagation can be through seeds or root division.

Zone 3-8

Bloom time: mid-late spring

BUTTERFLY FAVORITE

Native Regions

23

Missouri evening primrose

Oenothera macrocarpa or Oenothera missouriensis

aka: ozark sundrops, glade lily,
Missouri primrose

OVERVIEW

This native has a footprint in the Midwest, though small, mostly around Missouri. Its short stems are densely covered with 5" long, narrow, lance-shaped leaves. The flowers themselves are a bright sunny yellow. The petals open in the late afternoon or early evening and fade by the next day, making it a "night-owl" of flowers. Its nocturnal activity gives it its name "evening primrose". Though the blooms don't last long, the plant itself produces flowers for a long time. It grows close to the ground in sprawling, fluffy clumps. This makes it perfect for rocky outcroppings or border edging.

GROWING NOTES

This is a plant that's drought tolerant, making it perfect for rock gardens and gravelly sandy soils, like it's native habitat. Make sure those areas are well-drained. This flower can handle light shade but gets better blooms in the sun. Propagation is best from seed or stem cuttings.

Zone 4-8

Bloom time: late spring to early fall

Native Regions

common blue violet

Viola papilionacea

aka: confederate violet, hooded blue violet, wood violet

OVERVIEW

So we have a love/hate relationship with violets at our house. If my husband knew that I put common blue violets in this book, he might ground me from gardening for the year. Truthfully, a "weed" is only a plant that's growing in a place that you don't want it to grow. That can absolutely be said of the common blue violet. Though a delicate, pretty plant, it is quite invasive. It often grows in lawns and places that it's not wanted. But this humble flower is actually quite fascinating, and much loved by pollinators. One unique aspect is that it blooms twice in a season with completely different flowers. The Latin name actually describes the butterfly look of its first blooms. That is because of the five winglike purple-blue or gray-blue petals sitting on 6 stems which make up its first flowers in the spring. The side petals on top have fuzzy beards and the broad bottom petal is marked with a purple stripe. The purple stripe is a marker to guide pollinator to the nectar. Once those blooms go to seed there's a second flush of flowers in summer. But the flowers look like closed buds on short stems under the leaves. So as invasive as it is, it does provide a lot of nourishment to our pollinators throughout the season. The flowers are accented by its well-known heart-shaped leaves that come up from the root system.

GROWING NOTES

Speaking from my own experience as I mentioned, it's a very aggressive, invasive plant that grows pretty much anywhere: sun. shade, dry, wet. It needs to be kept in check if you put it in your garden. It can be kept at bay with taller plants growing nearby competing for sun and water. Propagation is from seed or rhizome division.

Zone 3-8

Bloom time: first in spring than in summer

Native Regions

snow-on-the-mountain

Euphorbia marginata

aka: mountain snow, variegated spurge

OVERVIEW

This native is loved by its foliage as much as its flowers. Its leaves are either a variegated light green or white with green striping, giving gardens great color and texture. The small white to light green flowers have five petals each. They look like tufts of snow, thus the name. This plant is also sought after because the blooms are very long-lasting, well into fall's first frost. It's one of the few natives that can grow in any cold zone, making it pretty unique and versatile. It self-sows from seed readily, year after year. It is an annual, but as long as it self sows its seeds, you'll get a new cycle of plants yearly

GROWING NOTES

Snow-on-the-mountain is actually a hardy plant and is very easy to grow. It can pretty much grow anywhere as long as there is sunshine. Propagation is best by seed, and as mentioned above, self-sows easily.

Zones: All zones

Bloom time: spring-early fall

Native Regions

FULL SUN

wild lupine

Lupinus perennis

aka: sundial lupine

OVERVIEW

This is a showy, often two-toned flower with blooming spikes. The lower level of blooms features blue blooms that turn a blue-purple, a blue-white or a pink-white closer to the top. The spike-like clusters are 8" long, and composed of individual flowers that are pea-shaped and 1" long. Complimenting the bold flower clusters are radiating, palm-shaped leaves. They are divided into seven to eleven leaflets, giving the whole plant a lot of eye-catching texture. The leaves follow the sun, thus the other common name "sundial lupine". Sadly, the plant goes dormant after it seeds in the summer. So be sure to garden plan later blooming plants around it to fill the visual "hole" it will leave in your garden. This is the host plant to the endangered Karner blue butterfly caterpillar. So planting wild blue lupine can really help this endangered species.

GROWING NOTES

Wild lupine prefers slightly acidic soil that's well-drained and moist. This plant can tolerate part shade. It is also drought tolerant and can handle sandier, harsher soils. Propagation is best by rhizome division or by seed.

Zone 3-8

Bloom time: late spring-early summer

Native Regions

31

FULL SUN

prairie onion
Allium stellatum

aka: autumn onion, pink wild onion, prairie wild onion

OVERVIEW

Alliums have earned their place among gardeners' wish lists because of their perky, round blooms. The prairie onion's flowers are often mistaken for chives. Its starry flower clusters come in pale pink to deep pink-purple, and sometimes white. Its 2" round flower "tufts" consist of small ¼" flowers with yellow centers. The blooms are unique in that they nod downward as they develop, like the nodding onion. But they perk up and stand erect as the flowers mature. The flowers sit atop a naked, long stem nestled among narrow grass-like leaf blades that are as tall as the plant. The leaves die back as the flower develops. So be sure to plan other plants around prairie onions to disguise the end of its life cycle. The plant does smell like onions.

GROWING NOTES

These natives are super flexible when it comes to tough growing conditions, such as dry, hot sunny areas, rock gardens, and hillsides. Its native habitats are dry prairies and rocky outcrops, so it is very hardy. That being said, it does like consistent, well-drained moisture. If it sits in standing water, the bulbs will rot. Propagation of the prairie onion is best by the division of the bulb clusters. Propagation by seed is also an option, and self sows readily in the wild, but starter plants take years to flower.

Zone: 5-9

Bloom time: mid-late summer

Native Regions

upland white aster

Solidago ptarmicoides

*aka: stiff aster, sneezewort aster, prairie aster,
upland white goldenrod*

OVERVIEW

This aster is actually a goldenrod. The botany world reclassified it after much disagreement. All because the flowers look like white asters and are quite daisy-like. But it is, in fact, a goldenrod, and a unique one, as it has creamy-white ray flowers. The blooming, flat-topped clusters consist of three to over twentyfive white blooms with yellow centers, each ½" in diameter. Basal leaves are green and oval and become more pointed and narrow the further up the plant they go. This plant is a late season bloomer. Its many flowers produce copious amounts of nectar for pollinators when it's scarce.

GROWING NOTES

This is an extremely hardy flowering native. It is native to rocky, dry and sandy soil so it is very drought tolerant. It can bloom and flourish in the hottest, driest of suns. This makes it a great candidate for rock gardens. It can tolerate some light shade, though. Propagation can be by seed or root division. But seeds are slow to germinate. Root division is the quickest and easiest way to propagate upland white asters.

Zone: 3-8

Bloom time: late summer-early fall

Native Regions

aromatic aster

Symphyotrichum oblongifolium

aka: fall aster, wild blue aster, shale barren aster

OVERVIEW

Let me start by saying that there are 200 varieties of wild asters. So this book is only scratching the surface of asters. This aster is aromatic, due to its leaves that release a balsam scent when crushed. The leaves are a deep blue-green, 4" long, rigid and dense, making the plant very compact and bushy. Flowers sprinkle the tops of these plants in blue, purple, pink or rose. No matter what color, they always have a yellow center, typical of asters. The small, daisy-like flowers are about 1" in diameter. They sit on erect, stiff stems. This aster is a more compact and bushier species than it's "leggier" aster cousins. It is also a late-comer to the "blooming party", being one of the last asters to bloom before the frost.

GROWING NOTES

A very easy grower, aromatic aster can flourish in the harshest conditions and are very drought tolerant. It can handle some shade, but when it is in a moist, well-drained area with plenty of sun, it will become quite aggressive. This plant is easily propagated by seed.

Zone: 4-7

Bloom time: late summer-early fall

BUTTERFLY FAVORITE

BEE FAVORITE

Native Regions

37

purple prairie clover
Dalea purpurea

aka: red tassel flower

OVERVIEW

This native plant holds a special place in my heart. It was the first native plant I purchased from the local forest preserve native plant sale, as a small baby. I had no idea what it was or what it was going to look like, and now it's one of my favorite flowers in my garden. It is such a unique plant with very unique leaves and a really interesting, distinct flower. The flowers look like little 2" prickly-grey cylinders, almost like mini cigars, before their bloom time. Then they explode with little $^{1}/_{4}$" flowers, often rose-purple to crimson. What gives this flower its most unique appearance is the way that it blooms. The blooms start at the base of the grey cylinder, in a flower ring. Then it slowly blooms upward until the whole cylinder is covered with pink blooms. Its fine, frilly-light 1" long leaflets making up fern-like leaves that dance around the base of the plant with much interest.

GROWING NOTES

This native plant prefers warm, moist soil with slight acidity. Yet, my own purple prairie clover is in alkaline soil and does very well. This native is drought tolerant, thanks to a deep taproot, and is best propagated from seed.

Zone: 3-8

Bloom time: summer

BEE FAVORITE

Native Regions

wild geranium

Geranium maculatum

aka: cranesbill, zonal geraniums

OVERVIEW

Sadly, wild geranium's flowers are somewhat short-lived. This is why wild geraniums are planted as much for its very distinct leaves as well as its flowers. The deeply cleft, large "palmate" leaves are cut into five to seven parts, with heavily-toothed edges. These leaves give the plant quite a presence in the garden. The delicate flowers range from a soft pink to rosy-lavender to bright white. All colors have bright yellow centers and look like pastel confetti in a garden bed. The 1½" wide flowers provide early nectar to pollinators. Once the flowers go to seed, the distinct leaves stay green throughout the season. This provides nice ground cover and foliage for the garden.

GROWING NOTES

This plant can tolerate part shade but it will produce more blooms, the more sun it receives. It's a very easy grower. It prefers fertile, moist, compost rich soil, like its native woodland habitat. Propagation is easily done by seed or root division. In fact, it self-sows easily if it's given enough space.

Zone 3-8

Bloom time: early-late spring to early summer

Native Regions

41

prairie smoke

Geum triflorum

aka: old man's whiskers, torch flower

OVERVIEW

This flower is one of the coolest ones in my sun bed. The nodding flowers look like buds that have not opened yet, and never bloom. The best part of this plant is when it goes to seed. The buds turn into clumps of feathery, plumed, pink-gray 2" "tails". Each filament holds a seed at the end. These plumes stand erect and sometimes bend to one side, looking like billowing smoke is waving in the wind. This is what inspires its common name. Flower colors range from a coral-red to a purple-red to a magenta-pink. My own plant has some lovely pinks and corals. Prairie smoke blooms in early spring and the seed plumes last well into summer. This provides an interesting texture and color for the first half of the growing season.

GROWING NOTES

This is a very forgiving plant, with a wide ability to handle a variety of soil conditions. It can tolerate alkaline and well-drained soil to poor, gravelly and acidic soil. This makes it a great plant to put anywhere and can be adaptable to rock gardens or dry, sandy areas. Propagation of this plant is best by seeds or rhizome division.

Zone 2-5

Bloom Time: late spring-early summer

Native Regions

43

FULL SUN

prairie coneflower

Ratibida columnifera

aka: red Mexican hat, upright coneflower,
Mexican hat, thimbleflower

OVERVIEW

'Mexican hat' is a perfect name for these bright, showy blooms. The 1-3" flowers are yellow or a two-toned red and yellow. The heads themselves look like droopy sombreros with dark purple-brown tops. The flowers start blooming at the base of the cylindrical cone at the center, with 3 to 7 petals. The leafless long stems make it a great cut flower for bouquets. Established plants can produce thousands of blooms, making a giant, floral firework display all summer. The flowers last throughout the growing season, well into the first frost of fall, making it a stable food source for pollinators.

GROWING NOTES

This plant, like many other coneflowers, are very adaptable to any soil. But it does prefer soil that is slightly alkaline. It is drought tolerant and very low maintenance, like its coneflower cousins. It propagates best by seed.

Zone 5-9

Bloom time: late spring to early fall

Native Regions

closed gentian

Gentian andrewsii

aka: bottle gentian, blind gentian

OVERVIEW

This plant is as interesting and exotic as it is easy to grow. The blossoms bunch themselves into 5-inch diameter clumps at the base of the upper leaves. The blooms themselves can be an intense navy blue to a blue-violet and sometimes even white. Attached to each flower is a petal-like 'pleat' that forms a 'tube'. So the flowers appeared to lack an opening to the flower and the pollen, thus the name 'closed', 'bottle' or 'blind'. Only larger, stronger bees, such as bumble-bees, can open the "curtain" and get into the flower to sip the nectar. Leaves are a narrow purple and grow either around the stem or opposite each other on the stem.

GROWING NOTES

This plant is very versatile about soil acidity and moisture. It can pretty much grow anywhere and can tolerate partial shade. Propagation is best by seed or root division. Germination from seeds is sometimes difficult.

Zone 3-6

Bloom time: late summer to fall

BEE FAVORITE

Native Regions

lance-leaved coreopsis

Coreopsis lanceolata

aka: sand coreopsis, tickseed

OVERVIEW

I propagated the tickseed in my garden through a seed packet I received from a cereal company promotion. My delicate tickseed reminds me of marigolds in a daisy-like form, and stay for a long time. The small, bright 2" flowers have eight daisy-like golden petals with a darker-red color at the base of each, surrounding a bright yellow disc. The happy flowers are effervescent with bright yellow and red, almost like a small, blooming circus. These small, sunny flowers last all summer, providing long lasting color. The leaves are deeply cut and lance shaped with a deep green color that accents their bright blooms. Tickseed makes a great cut flower for indoor bouquets.

GROWING NOTES

This is another very versatile native flowering plant that can handle moist to dry soil and tolerates dry conditions. It is easy to care for and practically grows anywhere. Propagation is through root division or seeds. I've had good luck with seeds and starter plants flower their first year.

Zone 4-9

Bloom time: late spring to summer

Native Regions

49

FULL SUN

meadow beauty

Rhexia virginica

aka: deergrass, Virginia meadow beauty, handsome Harry, meadow pitchers

OVERVIEW

This plant is often called deergrass because deer love it as a food source. Definitely one of the more exotic looking natives. Its $1^1/2$" delicate flowers feature rose crimson petals that explode around a ring of golden curved stamens. Complimenting it's bright jewel tones are light green leaves. It can be found in the Midwest even though it more abundantly found in the Southeast regions of the country.

GROWING NOTES

This plant like wet, acidic soil that aligns with its native habitat of marshy or boggy areas. This plant can tolerate part shade. It can withstand cold snaps in colder zones. It is best propagated by seed or tuber division.

Zones 5-9

Bloom time: midsummer to early fall

Native Regions

black-eyed Susan

Rudbeckia hirta

aka: brown-eyed Susan

OVERVIEW

Black-eyed Susans are a staple of Midwest gardens because of its low maintenance qualities and very long bloom time. Just walk around a flower-loving gardener's yard and you'll see plenty of black-eyed Susans. Blooms say "Summer is here!" and can last all summer long, even into early fall. This gives your garden plenty of bright yellow color. Black-eyed Susans are part of the sunflower family, and its golden-yellow ray flowers contain anywhere from ten to twenty petals each. The petals surround a chocolaty-brown center. The centers remind me of chocolate truffles setting atop bursts of yellow sunshine. Its long stems make for an attractive cut flower, too.

GROWING NOTES

This flower is extremely flexible which is why it is often planted by many gardeners. It can tolerate many soil conditions as well as periods of drought, but consistent watering is important. Propagation is easiest by seed and self-sows easily.

Zone: 3-9

Bloom time: summer-early fall

Native Regions

53

FULL SUN

prairie coral bells

Heuchera richardsonii

aka: alum root, prairie alumroot

OVERVIEW

This native version of coral bells features flowers that are green to creamy white. This differs from the white-pink flowers of its cultivar cousins. The basal leaves form a clump about 12"-18" tall. The leaves have white or purple bluish marbling on the leaves, giving it a very distinct look. Open, wiry stems shoot up from the base featuring tiny, delicate greenish-white bell-shaped flowers. This is a humble and unassuming plant. But the flowers are long-lasting. And when the flowers die back, the basal leaves add some interesting texture to your garden bed. Because of this, it can make a great ground cover.

GROWING NOTES

Native coral bells are an easy, low-maintenance grower. It prefers well-drained, moist soil. It can tolerate part shade and drought. But if things get too hot in warmer climates, it may dry out too fast, so mulch is advised. Propagation is best by root division.

Zone: 3-9

Bloom time: mid-summer

Native Regions

maypops

Passiflora incarnata

aka: purple passionflower, true passionflower, wild apricot, wild passion vine

OVERVIEW

I don't know how I have lived most of my gardening life without knowing about this fantastic flowering vine. These flowers are so unique and tropical looking, it had to be one of the flowering vines that made it into this book. Beyond its dramatic look, it earned a spot on these pages because pollinators-especially butterflies-love it. Each flower has a crown of fringe. This accents a lower layer of ray petals that angle down and out, like a ballerina's tutu. The fringe and petals surround a center of erect and distinct stamens and pistils. Blooms are usually white or lavender and edged with a darker purple. They are reminiscent (and related) to the cultivar passionflower. The 2"-3" flowers produce a fruit that if stepped on, makes a popping noise, thus the name. The vine features finely serrated leaves with three to five deep lobes. They give the vine a lot of depth once the flowers die back. It's a great candidate for quickly covering gates or training on trellises.

GROWING NOTES

This fast-growing perennial is very hardy, despite looking so tropical and delicate. Maypops like moist, rich, well-drained soil. It's very flexible with soil pH and texture- in fact, it can flourish in clay. The vine can handle light shade as well. But if you need a more shade tolerant version, look to Passiflora Leah. It has yellow colored flowers and is more shade tolerant. Maypops can be propagated by seed but germination may take years. A quicker way to propagate this plant is by cuttings or division of the roots. It is important to note that in colder zones, the plant dies to the ground and comes back with new shoots every spring. In warmer zones, the plant will become woody and new growth will be off of the old wood, like some clematises.

Zone: 5-9

Bloom time: early summer

BUTTERFLY FAVORITE

Native Regions

silky aster

Symphyotrichum sericeum

aka: western silvery master, mouse-eared aster

OVERVIEW

This aster gets its name from the hairy surface on its leaves that are silver-green in color, giving the leaves a silky feel. The numerous 1" long leaves are only outnumbered by the small clusters of bright flowers, each being ½" to 1 ½" in diameter. The flowers themselves are a daisy-like flower. They feature either deep lavender or light blue ray petals that surround bright yellow centers. The petals are long and thin, with a smooth appearance.

GROWING NOTES

Another versatile native, it naturally prefers drier, rockier and sandy conditions. This aster is also a slower grower than its cousins. It can tolerate partial shade and is easily propagated by seeds or root division.

Zone 3-8

Bloom time: late-summer-early fall

BUTTERFLY FAVORITE

BEE FAVORITE

Native Regions

nodding wild onion

Allium cernuum

aka: wild onion, lady's leeks

OVERVIEW

The flowers on this versatile plant tend to be light lavender in color but can also be pink or white. Around the base of the bulbs are soft, grass-like leaves. The flower clusters at the top of thin stems hang over and nod down toward the ground. These drooping clusters are what give the plant the name "nodding wild onion". The strong lines of the stems and leaves give gardens a nice, upright texture and structure.

GROWING NOTES

In general, this plant is easy to care for and very flexible. It is native to moist habitats, so it will thrive best in moist, well-drained soil. It can tolerate various soil acidity and is a great candidate for a rock garden. It can handle drought well. It also can tolerate some shade, but blooms will be slightly smaller and stunted. Propagation of this plant is usually through bulb division and can also be from seed. However, I have had little luck propagating any alliums from seed. Division of the bulb offsets and transplanting them in early spring is best. This is a good practice to do on occasion regardless, to prevent overcrowding.

Zone 4-8

Bloom time: midsummer

DYK?

Robert LaSalle, the famous explorer, marked on his map of the southwest shore of Lake Michigan an area where he saw a lot of nodding wild onions growing in the shallow water. He used the Algonquin Indians name 'chicagou' to do so. In time, the settlement that grew there was named Chicago, aligning with the map notation, thus naming the country's 'second city' after a humble onion.

Native Regions

smooth aster

Symphyotrichum laevis

OVERVIEW

Asters are always a great late-season flower. They provide color in your garden when all else is dying back for the winter. They can handle some early frost, which is a plus. And butterflies love it as in nectar source late in the season, and smooth aster is no different. It's called smooth aster because of it's smooth leaves, lacking the fine, rough hairs typical of asters. These leaves have a lovely bluish-green cast, accenting the bright blue flowers. Each little blue flower is about ¾" to 1¼" in diameter and has bright yellow centers. These attractive and numerous ray petal flowers are often a bright blue-purple but can sometimes be white. I enjoy these flowers on my fall morning walks at a local park. This amazing park focuses on native prairie flowers. Flanking many of its paths are tumbling purple "flower walls" of aster. Butterflies flit around everywhere, grabbing that much needed late-season food. Together they steal the show from the changing leaves of the trees.

GROWING NOTES

Like many asters, smooth aster is very flexible about soil as long as it's well-drained and moist. It's also a pretty drought tolerant flower. It blooms in September. Propagation is best by seeds or by cuttings, and self-sows readily.

Zone 3-8

Bloom Time: late summer-early fall

BEE FAVORITE

Native Regions

63

TALL HEIGHT
12"–48" (2 feet–4 feet) High

FULL SUN

wild bergamot

Monarda fistulosa

aka: bee balm, horsemint

OVERVIEW

This native is a gardener's favorite for many reasons. The first being its exotic looking blooms, that feature tufts of "hair" arching over tubular flowers. If Einstein became a punk rock flower, this would be it. The lavender-lilac, pink, white or fuchsia flowers sit in bunches atop two to four feet high stems. Complimenting these flowers are 3" long, grey-green leaves. This flower draws a copious amount of pollinators. Part of the reason may be its aromatic foliage that smells like the bergamot orange tree.

GROWING NOTES

Wild bergamot is native to dry prairies. So it is very drought resistant and doesn't need much moisture. It also can tolerate some shade. It can be propagated from seeds easily or by cuttings. In optimal conditions, it can get aggressive, so division of the plant may be necessary every few years.

Zone: 3-9

Bloom time: summer

BUTTERFLY FAVORITE

BEE FAVORITE

Native Regions

65

button liatris

Liatris aspera

aka: tall blazing star, button snakeroot, button blazing star, rough blazing star, rough gay father

OVERVIEW

'Button' is in its name because of the flower clumps or tufts that look like buttons along the spikes of flowers. Each flower spike holds 6" to 18" flowers that range from pink to lavender and sometimes white. They look like little 1" pom-poms. The flowers actually bloom from the top down in mid-summer. The showy flower spikes sit atop strong stems. Thin hairs, as well as short, narrow grass-like leaves, cover the stems.

GROWING NOTES

This plant prefers medium dry soil and tolerates some shade but does better in full sun. This plant is native to dry prairies so it does tolerate drought and unforgiving, sandy soil. It's propagated best by seed or root division.

Zone: 3-8

Bloom time: midsummer early fall

BUTTERFLY FAVORITE

BEE FAVORITE

Native Regions

dotted horsemint

Monarda punctata

aka: spotted bee balm, spotted horsemint, horsemint

OVERVIEW

This interesting native plant looks like a flower that could be found in a Dr. Seuss book. Being part of the bee balm family, it already has an exotic look. But dotted horsemint takes it to the next level-literally. This flower has a double-decker level of tubular flowers, creating a "pagoda" looking structure. The flowers are small and compact, forming a 2" to 3" creamy-white cluster. The flowers are spotted delicately with deep purple. Then, below and above the flowers, like a dress and a hat, are pink to green "bracts". These resemble pointed petals, making this plant quite a show-stopper. Adding to the sensory circus are purple-tinged stems that hold narrow, lance-shaped leaves that smell like oregano.

GROWING NOTES

This plant is very drought tolerant as it is used to sandy habitats. But it does prefer well-drained, moist soil. Propagation can be by seed or cuttings, though seeded starter plants take a long time to flower. In optimal conditions with consistent water, this plant can be aggressive. Dividing it from time to time might be prudent.

Zone: 4-9

Bloom time: mid-summer

BUTTERFLY FAVORITE

Native Regions

FULL SUN

New England aster

Symphyotrichum novae-angliae

aka: michaelmas daisy

OVERVIEW

Out of the hundreds of native asters, this is a giant in size, being large and shrubby with densely-packed hairy leaves. This native plant has a wide growing region far beyond New England. It produces clusters of flowers at the tips of the branches late in the season. This provides plenty of sweet nectar to pollinators as other flowers are dying back. The violet purple ray flowers surround a yellow gold center. It's very tolerant of frosts, allowing flowers to bloom well into fall. The stems themselves don't have many leaves, making them an attractive cut flower for indoor bouquets.

GROWING NOTES

New England aster is a flexible grower, adept at both alkaline or acidic soils. It does enjoy areas that are moist and well-drained, so you may need to mulch in dry areas during droughty conditions in the summer. It can tolerate partial shade. It can be propagated by cuttings, seed or root division.

Zone: 3-7

Bloom time: late summer to fall

BUTTERFLY FAVORITE

BEE FAVORITE

Native Regions

71

yellow coneflower
Ratibida pinnata

OVERVIEW

This native plant is another "bread-and-butter" gardening favorite. Gardeners use it for filler in many garden beds because of its bright colors and versatility. Another bonus is that it's a long bloomer. Flowers feature thirteen long, narrow, bright yellow drooping ray flowers circling a prominent cone-shaped center. Blooms bob on top of thin stems. The thin stems and drooping petals give the plant a delicate appearance as it dances in the breeze. It's also referred to as "gray-headed" because the center cones start the season as a medium gray color. Centers turn into a deep purplish-brown as the plant matures. These flowers are complemented by coarse, rough leaves divided into thin leaflets.

GROWING NOTES

This plant pretty much survives almost anything a gardener can throw at it-another reason for its popularity. It can flourish in drought conditions, and in rocky soils, and can tolerate light shade. But if you want to give it a happy home, it prefers well-drained soil with consistent moisture and some nice sun. It is propagated best by seed as well as root division. Seeds easily germinate and will bloom in their second year.

Zone: 3-9

Bloom time: midsummer to early fall

Native Regions

stiff goldenrod
Oligoneuron rigidum (originally Solidago rigida)

OVERVIEW

Open the door of goldenrod species and you will go down a deep rabbit hole. There are many different kinds of goldenrods and I'm just scratching the surface of this species in this book. Stiff goldenrod earned its place here because it attracts quite a few pollinators. It also isn't as invasive as other goldenrods. It's called stiff goldenrod because it stems are rigid, strong and very upright. Its stiff stems don't need any staking. Its leaves are soft, hairy and floppy at first, but as the plant matures the leaves become firm and stiff as well. Its large stalks feature large clusters of beautiful, bright yellow flowers that bloom late in the season. The great thing about goldenrods, in general, is that they give pollinators a lot of food late in the season.

GROWING NOTES

Stiff goldenrod is flexible on soil pH but does need moderate moisture and well-drained soil. It can handle sandy soil and droughty periods on account of its deep roots. Propagation of this plant is best by seed and self sows itself easily. In fact, seed propagation is the best approach. Its deep roots make it very difficult to transplant established plant divisions.

Zone: 3-9

Bloom time: late summer to fall

Native Regions

showy goldenrod
Solidago speciosa

OVERVIEW

Named showy goldenrod, this native lives up to its name with its "showy", frothy yellow clusters of flowers. The blooms create dense blooming "wands" or "spikes". These flowering 12" long plumes sit atop stiff, reddish-green stems. They make the plant feel very erect with good posture. This is different than typical goldenrod, whose flower clusters slope down lazily. Also unlike stiff goldenrod, showy goldenrod's 6" stems are shorter and smoother. It features alternating leaves, about 6" long, making this a shorter and more compact goldenrod.

GROWING NOTES

Showy goldenrod prefers dry to medium, well-drained soil. But it actually handles really poor soil, which can include clay, sand or rock. It can also tolerate part shade, unlike a lot of goldenrods. It is also very drought tolerant, making it a very easy grower. So basically, it can grow almost anywhere. Propagation is best by seeds but can be done through root division.

Zone: 3-8

Bloom time: midsummer to early fall

BUTTERFLY FAVORITE

BEE FAVORITE

Native Regions

Western sunflower

Helianthus occidentalis

aka: naked sunflower

OVERVIEW

The sunflower family is wide-ranging with many species. In fact, you could probably write a book dedicated to sunflowers alone. The Western sunflower is one of the shortest in height of the sunflower family. Its stems are stiff and leafless, making it a great cut flower. Each stem features loosely branched clusters of flower heads at the top. Those branches grow anywhere from 1 to 12 flowers. Each flower is 2" in diameter with a bright yellow center and surrounded by bright orange ray petals. At its base, there's a circle of oblong leaves forming a large clump, with leaf blades reaching 2-7" in length.

GROWING NOTES

This sunflower enjoys medium, well-drained soil, but it pretty much grows anywhere. It can even thrive in terrible dry, rocky or sandy soil. This sunflower can actually handle some light shade, too. And it is also quite a drought tolerant plant. So if you have a brown thumb, this sunflower might give you some growing confidence! It's not as aggressive a grower as other sunflowers, which makes it ideal for smaller gardens. Propagation is best by seed or root division. In fact, in optimal conditions, it self-sows easily.

Zone: 4-8

Bloom time: late summer-early fall

BEE FAVORITE

Native Regions

anise hyssop

Agastache foeniculum

aka: lavender hyssop, blue giant
hyssop, licorice mint

OVERVIEW

This plant's claim to fame is its dense spikes of lavender to purple flowers. The clusters grow close together on sturdy, erect stems. It's a showy flower, with small, tubular flowers filling the erect spike. It blooms all summer with long-lasting color. It then provides plenty of nectar for pollinators during the whole growing season. Its leaves are what gives it the "anise" or "licorice" name. They give off the scent of licorice when crushed.

GROWING NOTES

This plant can be a very aggressive grower. This is partly because it can grow in full sun to deeper shade, making it very flexible. It can also tolerate sandy, dry soil as well as well-drained, moist loamy soil. Moral of the story, it can grow anywhere. It self propagates by seed and will bloom within the first year of the starter plants. You can also propagate through dividing the rootstock. But you won't need to if you harvest its seeds and use its seeds to grow more. In fact, my native plant-loving friend graciously harvested an envelope-full of seeds for me. They all came up and bloomed the first year, attracting many bees and butterflies to my garden.

Zone: 3-8

Bloom time: all summer to early fall

BEE FAVORITE

BUTTERFLY FAVORITE

Native Regions

FULL SUN

showy tick trefoil

Desmodium canadense

OVERVIEW

The common name for this plant comes from a variety of things. First of all the name 'tick' comes from the look of the seeds themselves, that look like small ticks. The towering spikes of hundreds of rose-purple to lavender nodding flowers put on quite a 'show'. And finally, the leaves are divided into three leaflets, called a 'trefoil'. The countless flowers, each about ½" long, are bee and butterfly magnets.

GROWING NOTES

Another versatile grower, this native plant is not fussy about soil, it can grow in part shade. It is extremely hardy. In fact, if it has everything it needs, it can be very aggressive and push out other flowers, so division or thinning may be necessary from time to time. It is easily propagated from seed.

Zone: 3-6

Bloom time: summer

BUTTERFLY FAVORITE

BEE FAVORITE

Native Regions

83

TALL HEIGHT
24"–50" (2 feet–5 feet) High

gayfeather
Liatris pycnostachya

aka: prairie blazingstar, thick-spike gay father,
button snakeroot

OVERVIEW

One look at these blooms in your garden and you'll see why the common name for this plant is gayfeather. The 12" long erect flowering spikes look like feathery, flowering plumes. They are reminiscent of some magical Harry Potter-esque pink wands. Tiny individual flower heads, each with 5 long, slender pointed petals fill the clusters to the brim. The flowers themselves can range from a lavender color to fuchsia pink, and anywhere between. The spikes sit atop heavy stems. Grass-like leaves closely cover the length of the stalk, giving it a bottle-brush appearance. The flowers are a favorite for bees. It's very long bloom time gives bees a lot to do throughout the summer.

GROWING NOTES

This is a very versatile plant and is very drought resistant. But if it had its way, it prefers moist well-drained soil. It prefers slightly acidic soil, but my own gayfeather plants are in normal, alkaline soil and they do fine. They do need staking at times if they get too tall and the stalks get spindly. My own gayfeather plants do need staking. Propagation is easy by seeds or transplanting the corms.

Zone: 3-9

Bloom time: midsummer to mid-fall

BEE FAVORITE

Native Regions

leadplant

Amorpha canescens

aka: downy indigo bush, false indigo, prairie shoestring, devil's shoestrings or buffalo bellows

OVERVIEW

This semi-woody, shrubby plant is a favorite of a wide range of bee species, butterflies, moths, and beetles. Its small flower clusters arrange themselves in 4"-6" spikes atop 3-foot stems. The violet-grey blooms resemble lavender but are actually part of the pea family. It's known for its very deep tap roots, which allow it to not only recover from fires but to tolerate drought conditions. The taproots were such a nuisance for early pioneer farmers trying to plow prairies for crops, they coined the plant "devil's shoestrings".

GROWING NOTES

This native plant is incredibly versatile and can handle any kind of soil, even rocky and sandy spots. It prefers full sun, yet it can tolerate part shade, though it won't bloom as well and may get spindly. It propagates by seed and cuttings. Keep in mind, this plant is slow to get established, and may not flower for a few years. But once it gets going, it runs.

Zone: 3-7

Bloom time: summer

BEE FAVORITE

Native Regions

purple coneflower
Echinacea purpurea

aka: black sampson, red sunflower

OVERVIEW

This flower is basically the bread-and-butter of Midwest gardens. You can't pass a Midwest garden without seeing a purple coneflower. This native plant comes in many lovely cultivars like "Green Twister and "Double Scoop Bubble Gum". But the native coneflower is very versatile and long blooming. Each plant has twelve to twenty deep purple-pink to crimson ray flowers. The blooms have drooping petals revolving around a rusty-golden 1" domed disc. These flowers are on tall stems which make it a great cut flower for indoor bouquets. This flower also has 3"-8" toothed leaves that are a rough dark green adding a nice texture to the plant. This is a long bloomer and as the plant matures through the season the petals droop more.

GROWING NOTES

There are many reasons purple coneflower is a favorite among gardeners. First, it is very drought tolerant, because of its fibrous root system that is very extensive. It grows anywhere in any kind of soil and any kind of moisture situation making it very low maintenance. Propagation can be through root division or seeds. The seeds germinate pretty easily and can grow first-year blooms.

Zone: 3-8

Bloom time: early summer to early fall

Native Regions

DYK?

"Echinacea" is a Greek word for 'hedgehog' and 'sea urchin' referring to the prickly domed disc at the center of the plant

butterfly weed

Asclepias tuberosa

aka: orange milkweed, butterfly plant, pleurisy root, chigger flower

OVERVIEW

As much as this is a butterfly favorite (thus the name) it is one of my own favorites, too. This plant bursts with long-lasting, bright orange flowers in mid-summer. My own butterfly weed is a bright sunset orange. But blooms can be a bright yellow-orange to a deeper red-orange color. The flat-topped clusters of flowers develop copious amounts of nectar and sticky pollen. The pollen attaches to insects' legs and feet, assuring pollination. It is also a larval food for some butterfly species, so you can see where it gets its common name. butterfly weed is part of the extensive milkweed family. But it's a smaller, more compact and delicate plant, in relation to other milkweeds.

GROWING NOTES

Butterfly weed is an incredibly versatile plant. It can handle drought pretty well and any kind of soil, but does prefer a sandier habitat. Propagation is best by seeds, as well as root cuttings. I propagated my own butterfly weed by seeds sown in late April outside and it bloomed that same year.

Zone: 3-10

Blooms: late spring-late summer

BUTTERFLY FAVORITE

Native Regions

prairie phlox
Phlox pilosa

aka: downy phlox

OVERVIEW

This plant is also considered downy phlox, coming from the Latin name pilosa. Short soft hairs on the leaves give this phlox a fuzzy soft texture, inspiring the pilosa name. A cacophony of flower clusters fill the tops of the long leafy stalks, giving your garden fireworks of color in early summer. This plant's flowers come in a wide range of colors, from lavender, light pink, rose pink or even white. Blooms release pollen several days before the stigmas can even receive it. This encourages the cross-pollination needed by butterflies and hummingbirds who visit this flower.

GROWING NOTES

Prairie phlox is an incredibly flexible, easy to grow plant. It pretty much can grow in any well-drained soil but does prefer sandier soil, like its native habitat. It propagates by seed as well as stem cuttings or even root division.

Zone: 3-8

Bloom time: mid spring-early summer

BUTTERFLY FAVORITE

Native Regions

marsh phlox

Phlox glaberrima

aka: smooth phlox

OVERVIEW

This phlox is referred to as smooth phlox because it stems and leaves are hairless. This is the main difference visually between this phlox and its cousins. Atop its stems are small, flat-topped clusters filled with three to twenty tubular blooms, each about ¾" in length. The flowers range from being reddish purple to pink and sometimes white. The flowers have an aromatic, sweet perfume, drawing many pollinators and gardeners alike. Marsh phlox boasts lance-shaped leaves, alternating up the stems. Stems are strong and erect and rarely need staking.

GROWING NOTES

Marsh Phlox, true to its name, is native to moist meadows and riverbanks. So it stands to reason that it prefers moist well-drained soil and does not do well in dry spells. Consistent moisture is key to a thriving colony of marsh phlox. Beyond its sensitivity to soil moisture, it can handle soil texture easier, including damp clay. It can also tolerate part shade locations. Propagation is best by seed or transplanting rhizome offshoots. In optimal conditions, it self sows by readily.

Zone: 3-8

Bloom time: mid to late spring

Native Regions

pasture rose

Rose carolina

aka: prairie rose, Carolina rose

OVERVIEW

We discovered this plant on our Michigan property, growing on a harsh, sandy slope with little sun. Though scruffy, I found some blooms on it. Surprisingly it was surviving its harsh environment. I transplanted it to a sunny well-drained corner of my garden. Since then, it has gifted me with many summer blooms. The 2" flowers have five pink petals that surround a ring of yellow stamens. These deliver copious amounts of pollen bees love. The seeds or "hips" stay on the plant through the winter and provide food for hungry wildlife.

GROWING NOTES

As you can tell from my story, this plant is very hardy. It tolerates dry sandy soil but will bloom and thrive in a moist well-drained corner of your garden. It can also handle being in part shade but again you'll get more vigorous growth and blooms if it receives more sun. Propagation is by seeds as well as cuttings and root division.

Zone: 4-9

Bloom time: late spring-early summer

BEE FAVORITE

Native Regions

97

wild quinine

Parthenium integrifolium

aka: American feverfew, Eastern feverfew, Eastern parthenium

OVERVIEW

The flower heads remind me of yarrow, except these flat-topped flower clusters are grayish-white in color. The flowers look like small buttons. But they are actually small ¼" little ray flowers surrounding a white dome. They grow in compact clusters, reminiscent of soft wool or puffy clouds. They sit atop stiff, erect stems that feature alternate leaves along the length of them. The stiff stems shoot up from a large clump of large toothed basal leaves that are 12" long. This plant boasts a long bloom time, giving gardeners and pollinators a lot to enjoy for a long time. This is another flower rarely found in its native habitat these days and endangered in some states. So planting one can make a big impact.

GROWING NOTES

This is a very hearty native perennial that can tolerate large swings in temperature. It thrives in fertile, well-drained soil. It can thrive in part shady conditions. Propagation is best by seeds.

Zone: 4-8

Bloom time: summer through autumn

Native Regions

FULL SUN

queen of the prairie
Filipendula rubra

aka: meadow-sweet

OVERVIEW

The explosive color on such a tall plant gives the presence and regalness that gives the plant its name. Its leaves have seven to nine deep lobes with an outer toothed edge giving it a nice texture. The leaves themselves can be 3 feet long. But its real claim to fame is the showy, flat-topped pink sprays of small, perfumed blossoms. The tufts of flower clusters usually span 4"-10"across. The clusters look like frothy pink sea foam, rolling atop a garden's back border. It's a late-season bloomer. So its a great addition for some long-lasting color in your garden when a lot of your other flowers have gone to seed.

GROWING NOTES

This plant is native to moister habitats, such as pond edges or moist meadows. So it does need moisture in your garden, but it definitely doesn't like standing water. It does like compost-rich soil and it's prudent to mulch this plant in colder zones. Propagation is very versatile, either by seeds, stem cuttings, and root division. But rootstock division is best for this plant.

Zone: 3-8

Bloom time: summer to early fall

Native Regions

culver's root

Veronicastrum virginicum

aka: culver's physic, bowman's root

OVERVIEW

Culver's root sounds like it should be a saloon in an old wild west movie. But the showy, bold flowers are anything but low-brow. The plant was named after a Dr. Culver, who used the root as a medicinal. Later, science showed that the root contained Leptandrin, a potential cathartic. Tiny, trumpet-shaped flowers cover tall spikes reminiscent of blooming bottle-brushes standing erect. The tiny flowers are either white or lavender and have four lobes and two stamens each. These flowers may be small, but contain a lot of sweet nectar that the bees go crazy for. An added plus of all that sweet nectar is that the flowers last a long time. This gives the bees a lot of food throughout the growing season. These large, spiky plants make quite a statement in a garden border. They are only enhanced by the 6" long lance-shaped, toothed edged leaves. The foliage provides nice texture once the flowers die back.

GROWING NOTES

This plant is adaptable and easy to grow, so if you have a brown thumb, this plant should be on your list. It thrives in average to damp soil. It prefers compost-rich soil but isn't fussy about soil's acidity. More mature, established plants tolerate drier conditions versus younger plants. Propagation can be from seed, stem cuttings or root division.

Zone: 3-8

Bloom time: summer-late summer

BEE FAVORITE

Native Regions

103

rattlesnake-master

Eryngium yuccifolium

aka: button snakeroot, yucca-leaf eryngo

OVERVIEW

This is a distinct, interesting plant with a distinct, interesting name. Yet it has no relation to snakes whatsoever. What gives the plant its unique look is it soft, compact flower heads that almost look like buttons. Each tiny flower covers each 1" diameter globule 'button' or 'globe', made up of five greenish-white petals that you can barely see. The incredibly aromatic flowers attract many pollinators, especially bees. Adding to its interesting look in the garden is it's spiny-edged, soft, thick leaves like yucca plants. These leaves can grow up to 3 feet in length at the base of the plant. Once the flowers have died back, the leaves offer some long-lasting texture and structure.

GROWING NOTES

This is a very hardy plant and can tolerate a wide range of soil from dry to moist. It's not fussy but does like a well-drained space. You can propagate this plant by seed but starter plants don't bloom until their second year. For quicker blooms rootstock division may be best.

Zone: 4-9

Bloom time: early-midsummer

BEE FAVORITE

Native Regions

FULL SUN

Joe-pye weed

Eupatorium purpureum

aka: sweet Joe pie weed

OVERVIEW

This plant has a large, showy dome of large rose to mauve colored flowers. It is a tall, erect plant, with 4 lance-shaped leaves circling the stem all the way up. Each flower cluster has 5 to 7 florets that are extremely fragrant, making it a butterfly magnet. In fact, some have noted the flowers smell like vanilla.

GROWING NOTES

Joe-pye weed prefers moist, well-drained soil and can handle some light shade. It's very low maintenance and easy to grow but does need a lot of space because of its girth. Some consider this plant a weed and prefer not to plant it. But it is very important to butterflies, so gardeners should find a roomy corner to plant one. It's very flexible when it comes to soil, being able to adapt to clay and alkaline soils. It propagates by seed readily and root division. But propagation is best by cuttings.

Zone: 4-8

Bloom time: midsummer to early fall

DYK?

This plant was named after Jopi-an (joe pye), an Indian medicine man who treated patients with this plant.

BUTTERFLY FAVORITE

Native Regions

compass plant

Silphium laciniatum

aka: rosinweed, Jack and the beanstalk

OVERVIEW

When considering the evolutionary relationship between native plants, its habitats, and its pollinators- look no further than the compass plant. It's sweet yellow ray flowers, 2" to 5" in diameter, rise high above the grassy plains, its native habitat. The height of these plants alert pollinators where the food source is above the prairie. Because of this, these plants can grow up to 6 feet high! You can see why Jack in the beanstalk is one of its common names. The blooms are long-lasting, giving bees an extra food source later in the season. To add to its bulky presence are large tufts of hairy green leaves, growing like a small mountain at the base. Leaf blades grow up to 2 feet in length. The other interesting thing about this plant is why it's called a compass plant. The sun can get pretty aggressive on the grassy plains. A compass plant's leaves point north and south, to avoid the heat of the noon-day sun, like a compass. (You have to love mother nature.) As an early pioneer, you could have used these plants for directions. When you do the math, 6 feet in height with leaves 2 feet long, means a large amount of space is needed for the spectacular plant. Look for an open, sunny corner or a roomy back area of a garden bed where you can use a compass plant's height and color.

GROWING NOTES

As I mentioned, the compass plant needs a lot of space to grow. It isn't fussy about soil and the taproot can go down to 15 feet, making it extremely drought tolerant. As long as it has the space it needs, this plant can be an easy addition to your yard. Plant propagation is easiest with seeds, and self sows readily.

Zone: 3-8

Bloom time: summer

BEE FAVORITE

BUTTERFLY FAVORITE

Native Regions

DYK?

Early Americans used the resinous sap for chewing gum

pentstemons

Penstemon digitalis

aka: foxglove beardtongue, white beardtongue

OVERVIEW

This flower is called beardtongue, because of its hairy stamen that sticks out of the white tubular flowers, looking like a tongue. The lip-like blooms sit atop tall flower stalks. They resemble snapdragons, as well as their cultivar cousins foxglove. But native penstemons are much heartier than the cultivar foxglove. The flower colors range from lavender, violet-purple, pink, blue and white. Basal leaves circle the stalks, which are shiny and toothed on the edges.

GROWING NOTES

Native penstemons tolerate light shade. They are flexible on the soil moisture, too, but needs good drainage. It self sows easily once established and can be propagated by dividing its roots as well.

Zone: 3-8

Bloom time: early spring

Native Regions

prairie ironweed
Vernonia fasciculata

aka: Western ironweed, common ironweed, smooth ironweed

OVERVIEW

This plant is called ironweed, in reference to its tough stem that holds large clusters of bright rose-purple to purple flowers. Its 6" long leaves are dark green and coarse toothed. The flower clusters are flat-topped, about 4" across, with smaller clusters below. Each cluster features ten to thirty tubular flowers. This native is a host plant to the American Painted Lady butterfly. So it's very important to our ecosystem as well as eye-popping lovely.

GROWING NOTES

At 2 to 5 feet tall, this plant needs a lot of space to grow. It prefers moister soils as it's native to marshes as well as prairies. It can adapt to average garden soil and can also handle part sun. If it has space and ideal conditions it can get aggressive. It propagates easily through seed. In fact, to manage it, deadheading spent flowers before going to seed is a prudent chore. Or you may have an ironweed forest before long.

Zone: 4-9

Bloom time: mid/late summer-early fall

BUTTERFLY FAVORITE

Native Regions

113

royal catchfly
Silene regia

OVERVIEW

"Regia" in Latin means regal, and once you see silene regia in its glory, you'll know why it was given that name. This show stopper when in bloom is covered in bright red flowers. Each bloom has 5 thin, pointed petals, about 2" in diameter that grow in small clusters. They cover stiff stems which also grow stalkless leaves all the way up its length. Its called catchfly because of its production of sticky glands that cause insects to get stuck to it. And as if this plant was created in some horror movie, it produces digestive enzymes too, to break down the dead insects. This prevents their decomposition to rot the plant. When mother nature thinks of everything, she thinks of everything! Beyond the random, small insects getting stuck on this plant, its flowers are a pollinator magnet. Hummingbirds and butterflies especially love it. This regal native is, unfortunately, becoming rare in the wild. In some states, it is listed as endangered.

GROWING NOTES

This plant is native to drier prairie habitats but adapts well to normal garden conditions. Because of its native proclivities, it's drought tolerant and can flourish in rockier, sandier spots. On the other side of the equation, it can tolerate part shade. However, more shade means it will become short-lived and the stalks won't be as strong. Propagation is best by root division or by seeds. In fact, it self-sows by seed readily.

Zone: 4-9

Bloom time: summer

Native Regions

false sunflower

Heliopsis helianthoides

aka: early sunflower, smooth sunflower, oxeye daisy

OVERVIEW

Although called sunflower, it is not considered a true sunflower. This is due to the fact its petals and centers create seeds. True sunflowers produce seeds only in their center discs. But like many sunflowers, this plant features 2"-4" yellow daisy-like flowers that bloom all summer long. The petal colors range from a deep golden yellow to an orange-yellow. Each erect flower cluster sits atop a stiff-branched stalk, sometimes featuring one flower or many. All blooms have bright yellow centers. In open areas, it can get quite bushy in appearance. Adding to its bushiness is its ovate, toothed, rough leaves, growing from $2^{1}/_{2}$"-5" long. Pollinators enjoy its pollen, nectar and its long bloom time.

GROWING NOTES

False sunflower can tolerate light shade. It prefers average, well-drained moist soil. Established plants are quite drought tolerant and can live in rocky, sandy, inhospitable areas. Propagation is best by seed and self sows easily. You can also propagate false sunflower by dividing large clumps of the rhizomes at the base and transplanting them.

Zone: 3-8

Bloom time: early summer-early fall

BEE FAVORITE

BUTTERFLY FAVORITE

Native Regions

117

swamp milkweed

Asclepias incarnata

aka: rose milkweed, pleurisy root, white Indian hemp

OVERVIEW

Similar to its cousins, this milkweed features large clusters of aromatic, rosy-red flowers. Flowers bloom in mid-summer on a rigid stalk. Florets can also come in a rarer white color and mauve colors. They have a long bloom time, which is fortunate for monarchs who love these plants. The flower clusters are complemented by dark green, lance-shaped leaves. Its common name refers to the silken strands that attach themselves to its seeds in the pods. When the pods begin to open to release the seeds the strands that wiggle their way out, look like dripping milk. Its common name also comes from its milky-white sap the plant releases when cut.

GROWING NOTES

It's called swamp milkweed because it is native to wet, swampy habitats. So it does prefer moist, humus-rich soil. That being said, it can adapt to normal garden conditions quite easily. It can tolerate some light shade. Due to its deep roots, their division is difficult. It is best propagated by seed.

Zone: 3-8

Bloom time: summer

BUTTERFLY FAVORITE

Native Regions

119

rose mallow

Hibiscus moscheutos

aka: crimson-eyed rose mallow, marshmallow hibiscus, swamp rose mallow

OVERVIEW

Rose mallow is a relative to hollyhocks and one look at its blooms and you'll see the resemblance. Pretend hibiscus, rose of Sharon and hollyhocks had a baby, and you have rose mallow. It's showy, five-petaled blooms range from red to pink to creamy white. They usually have a band of red at the base and in the center, where it also features a long, distinct stamen. This plant looks like it belongs in warmer, tropical climates. It is slow to come out of its winter sleep in the spring, but once it wakes and the heat of summer kicks in, so does rose mallow. The 5" wide flowers last only for a day, but the plant produces many during its bloom time. Flowers sit atop sturdy stems that are densely packed, making it a shrubby perennial. Along the stems are 6" long serrated fuzzy green leaves.

GROWING NOTES

Rose mallow is native to wetlands and marshes so it prefers moisture. It can transition to regular garden environments but does need consistent moisture, especially on hot days. It can tolerate pretty much anything you can throw at it; part shade, clay soil, standing water. Propagation is best by seed or root division.

Zone: 5-9

Bloom time: midsummer early fall

Native Regions

121

cow parsnip

Heracleum maximum

aka: common parsnip, Indian celery, Indian rhubarb

OVERVIEW

Cow parsnip is the cousin of the toxic, invasive non-native giant hogweed. Hogweed causes severe burns and blisters, so please don't confuse the two. Cow parsnip, however, is a native plant that pollinators of all shapes and sizes adore for its copious amounts of nectar. The amount of nectar is thanks to all the numerous small white or pale pink flowers it produces. At first glance, this plant looks like it has cluster upon cluster of tiny flowers. In fact, each large cluster is made up of fifteen to thirty smaller clusters of thirty flowers each! It's a bloom-a-palooza! Each tiny little flower is about a $^1/_4$" in diameter with five petals and loads of nectar. The large basal leaves are 18" long, palmated with three soft and hairy lobes. Though a biannual, cow parsnip reseeds itself so aggressively after it's first year, it feels like a perennial.

GROWING NOTES

Cow parsnip is an easy flexible grower that likes medium moisture and well-drained soil. It can tolerate part shade spots, too. It can get invasive in optimal growing conditions so it may need to be thinned or divided periodically. Similar to its cousin, the giant hogweed (but not as extreme), its sap can cause skin sensitivity. Be sure to wear gloves when handling this native. This plant needs a bit of space, as it can grow to 10 feet high. Propagation is best by seeds, and self sows readily on its own given space. You can also divide the roots, just take care to not touch the sap.

Zone: 3-9

Bloom time: late spring-early summer

Native Regions

124

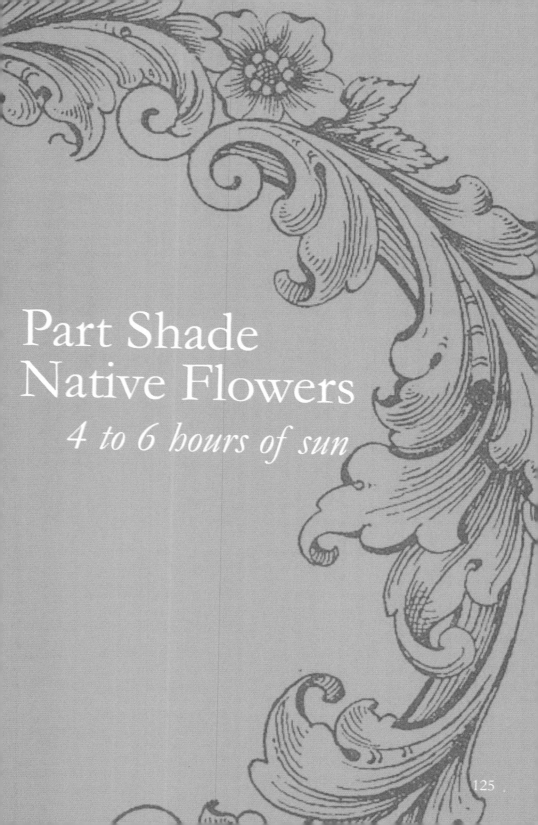

Part Shade
Native Flowers
4 to 6 hours of sun

bird's foot violet

Viola pedata

aka: pansy violet

OVERVIEW

This spring to early summer bloomer gets its name from its bird feet shaped leaves. This is because the leaves, which are ¾ to 2" long have deep three to five segments. Bright flowers each with five petals dot these low, compact plants. The flowers contain a brilliant orange color at the center, contrasting with the ranges of purple typical of violets. Those purples can range in color from a pale blue-lavender to a dark purple.

GROWING NOTES

Bids foot violet is a very versatile plant, and does well in many soil scenarios; from well-drained, loamy soil to sandy, gravelly soil. It can live in brighter or shadier spots. Its only nuance is that it prefers soil that is not too wet. Propagation is best from seed as well as root cuttings

Zone: 3-8

Bloom time: spring- early summer

Native Regions

Allegheny spurge

Pachysandra procumbens

aka: mountain spurge

OVERVIEW

This plant is sought after for its greenery as much as its flowers. The flowers grow in pinkish white to greenish white, in spiky fragrant clusters. The flower clusters sit atop unique scalloped gray-green leaves with sometimes lighter mottling. The mottling is reminiscent of a Pollack painting. The plants themselves are shrubby and low-growing, forming a dense carpet for shadier spots. The leaves are evergreen in warmer zones, making for great all year round color and texture in some states. This is a slower grower than its cousin the Japanese spurge. I am always yanking chunks of Japanese spurge out of my garden beds because it's so aggressive. Allegheny spurge has a more delicate look and texture and isn't as aggressive.

GROWING NOTES

Being a woodland native, this plant prefers a humus rich, well-drained, moist soil. It is also tolerant of a deeper shade. Established plants are drought tolerant in cooler climates. Occasional thinning of established plant colonies may be necessary to keep good air circulation. This causes better growth and blooms. Propagation is best by stem cuttings or rhizome division.

Zone: 4-9

Bloom time: spring

Native Regions

green and gold

Chrysogonum virginianum

aka: golden star, golden knee

OVERVIEW

This is a great native to put in front of your beds or to line a path because it's low-growing and compact. Its leaves are semi-evergreen, fuzzy green and oval-shaped, about 1"-3" in length. Bright yellow blooms feature five delicate little ray petals that grow around a tiny bouquet of small, brown centers. They look like 1½" golden stars scattered among the greenery. New flowers bloom all through the growing season. This gives gardens plenty of color and pollinators plenty to do.

GROWING NOTES

Green and gold is native to woodlands, so it likes moisture and some shade. It does need at least half a day of sun, so it can tolerate part shade as long as it gets in the sunshine. It can also tolerate sunnier spots, but it needs consistent moisture in those areas to thrive. This low grower is a great plant for rock gardens. It's very drought tolerant and flexible with soil pH. Propagation can be done by seed as well as cuttings and root division. It colonizes on its own by creeping rhizomes along the ground, making for good ground cover. But it is not as aggressive a grower as others.

Zone: 5-9

Bloom time: spring-late summer

Native Regions

wintergreen
Gaultheria procumbens

aka: teaberry, checkerberry

OVERVIEW

This plant made its way to the Midwest edition because its native to Wisconsin and Minnesota. This aromatic ground cover trails along the forest floor. Its semi-woody stems rise 2"-4" above the ground. Its waxy, thick, evergreen leaves do smell like wintergreen-mint. Each stem produces one to two nodding white flowers about ½" long. Each flower looks similar to an urn, with five lobes that dangle below the leaves.

GROWING NOTES

As a woodland native plant, it prefers slightly acidic soil with plenty of organic material mixed throughout. Though it is generally pretty flexible and an easy grower. It prefers partial shade but can tolerate deeper shade. Wintergreen is best propagated by splitting the runners and transplanting them. Propagation can be by seed. However, its seeds germinate slowly.

Zone: 3-7

Bloom time: summer

Native Regions

bunchberry

Cornus canadensis

aka: dwarf cornel, crackerberry, pudding berry, creeping dogwood

OVERVIEW

Bunchberry is a relative to the dogwood tree, but it is very low growing making perfect groundcover. It is a favorite for shady gardens, because of its small greenish-white blooms in the late spring. The creamy white 'petals' are not petals at all, but 'bracts', which fall away once the flowers turn into berries. At the center of the bracts are the true flower, consisting of small yellow stamens and dark brown styles. (Yes, get your botany books out!) This 1" bunchberry bloom cluster gives the plant a unique look. The cluster is nestled in a circular nest of four to six tapered oblong leaves that turn a deep wine-red color in the fall. It is found mostly in the upper Midwest regions of the country.

GROWING NOTES

Bunchberry is another native woodland plant that prefers cool, moist, slightly acidic soil. It also likes mulch in the fall, like its native home. It can tolerate sunnier locations, but its growth will become stunted. Propagation is best by seed or rhizome division.

Zone: 1-6

Bloom time: late spring-early summer

Native Regions

135

wild lily-of-the-valley

Maianthemum canadense

*aka: false lily-of-the-valley, Canada mayflower,
two-leaved Solomon's seal, bead ruby*

OVERVIEW

Though lily-of-the-valley is in this plant's name, it looks very different from true lily-of-the-valley. True lily-of-the-valley features small bell flowers. False lily-of-the-valley flowers look like flowery feathers. The 1"-2" long plumes of $^1/_4$" flowers each have two small petals, usually white or cream in color, and are very fragrant. They remind me of sparklers or fireworks during a 4th of July celebration. The flowers produce edible berries which become a food source for many small, woodland animals. This then allows the plant to propagate far and wide through the animals' digestive tracts.

GROWING NOTES

Native to woodlands, it likes loamy, moist soil that's mildly acidic. It is very adaptable and can tolerate full sun as well as part shade. Yet you will get larger flowers in part shade. This plant is easily propagated by rhizome division. It can also be propagated by seeds, but germination and flowering take longer.

Zone: 2-7

Bloom time: mid-late spring

Native Regions

bellwort

Uvularia perfoliata

aka: perfoliate bellwort, mealy bellwort, merrybells

OVERVIEW

This woodland native has very interesting leaves. Shooting up from the base of the plant are stems that look like they're jutting through the leaves themselves as if the stem is piercing through them. The stem gets forked near the top. Each side features a bell-shaped, light yellow flower dangling from it as if weeping. This plant comes in a few variations with size and leaf shapes. For larger flowers, there's a "large-flowered bellwort". Bellwort is becoming rare to find in its woodland habitat. Large-flowered bellwort is now endangered in some eastern states. If you find it in the woods; take a picture, post it on Instagram, thank the flower Gods, and (please) leave it untouched.

GROWING NOTES

Bellwort is native to woodlands, so it prefers moist, rich soil that is well-drained. This plant can tolerate deeper shade but not very deep shade. It is best propagated by rhizome division but can be by seeds as well.

Zone: 4-8

Bloom time: end of spring early summer

Native Regions

dwarf crested iris

Iris cristata

OVERVIEW

Part of the iris family, this native is actually smaller and more compact than other irises. It's shorter stature makes it a great candidate for unique ground cover. The stiff, yellow-green colored sword-shaped leaves stand erect at 6". The leaves surround a flower stalk carrying a pale blue, lilac or lavender flower. This iris spreads easily and quickly, creating a purple carpet when in bloom.

GROWING NOTES

The dwarf crested iris prefers moist well-drained soil like its woodland home. That being said, it can thrive in rock gardens and on drier slopes. It can tolerate sunnier spots, too, as long as there is consistent moisture. Propagation is best by rhizome division because seedlings take about two to three years to flower.

Zone: 3-9

Bloom time: mid spring

Native Regions

false rue-anemone

Isopyrum biternatum

OVERVIEW

The world of anemones is wide and deep. It includes many different species; rue anemone, woodland anemone, Canada anemone. I included this anemone because of its favor among bees who collect its pollen. This woodland flower is often mistaken for Rue (true) anemone. False rue has five sepals (that look like petals) and true rue has six to twelve. This early spring bloomer features 1" loose, waxy-white floral clusters with bright yellow centers. The yellow-green leaves look similar to Columbine and are divided into three segments, then again into three leaflets. The basal leaves are evergreen. This lovely bloom is becoming
endangered in some states.

GROWING NOTES

This woodland plant is low-lying, making it perfect for rock gardens and rocky slopes. Because it is a native woodland plant, it likes rich, moist slightly acidic soil. It can grow in deeper shade. Propagation can be from root division or seeds.

Zone: 4-8

Bloom time: early spring

BEE FAVORITE

Native Regions

cutleaf toothwort

Dentaria laciniata

aka: crow's toes, pepper root

OVERVIEW

This woodland native is a very early bloomer. These plants give much-needed nectar to pollinators early in the growing season. Delicate clusters of white with light pink edges, four petaled flowers sit on 6"-12" smooth stems. The flowers tend to be floppy but become perkier and more erect on sunnier days. Leaves are palmate with three to four very narrow leaflets with heavily-toothed edges. In fact, they almost look like cannabis leaves! This flower is very delicate. When the invasive "garlic mustard" invades an area, this is one of the first plants to decline in numbers.

GROWING NOTES

As a woodland native, it prefers humus-rich, moist, well-drained soil. However, it is very flexible with normal garden soil if need be. This flower thrives in part shade, as too much sun yellows the leaves. Propagation can be by root division and by seeds. In fact, seed propagation is quite easy and self sows readily in ideal growing conditions.

Zone: 3-8

Bloom time: early spring

Native Regions

Dutchman's breeches

Dicentra cucullaria

aka: little blue staggers, bleeding heart

OVERVIEW

One look at this plant and you know why it's called Dutchman's breeches. The name describes its distinct creamy-white flowers dangling on a 12" long stem. They look like clusters of doll-sized, Victorian pantaloons, hanging upside down drying on a clothesline. Generally found in the woods, this wildflower blooms in early to mid spring. The blooms consist of two white spur petals facing upward with a yellow cream opening at the center. Sometimes the white flowers will have a slight pink hue. The gray-green leaves at the base have a fern-like appearance. This plant likes to be pollinated particularly by queen bumblebees.

GROWING NOTES

Being woodland plants, it likes humus rich soil that's moist and well drained. It can tolerate deeper shade. It's best propagated by tuber division and can be propagated by seeds. However, seeds do take a while for the plant to germinate and flower. They are known to self sow themselves, slow as the process is.

Zone: 3-7

Bloom time: early spring-mid spring

Native Regions

shinleaf

Pyrola elliptica

aka: waxflower shinleaf

OVERVIEW

Shinleaf is treasured among gardeners because it blooms during the middle of summer, in shadier spots. This is usually difficult for shade plants. It also gives you a dark green color all year long because the plants is an evergreen. The leaves are clustered in a rosette arrangement at the base of the plants and are elliptical in shape. The slender flower stalk is 4"-12" high. Climbing up the stalk, like a spiral staircase, are anywhere from three to twentyone nodding, fragrant white flowers. Their petals are either tinged with pink or veined with green, giving unique color to a shady corner. The flowers each have five petals about $1/3$" long. The style at the center, hangs down past the petals, looking like a parasol handle. This gives the blooms a playful look.

GROWING NOTES

Shinleaf is another woodland wildflower that grows best with organic material mixed into the soil such as compost, and peat moss. It is flexible with soil moisture. An addition of conifer leaves to its habitat makes it's native home more acidic, which shinleaf prefers. This plant is tough to propagate from seed because they are slow to germinate. So it's best to divide its runners to propagate this plant.

Zone: 2-6

Bloom time: summer

BEE FAVORITE

Native Regions

wild leek

Allium trioccum

aka: ramp, three-seeded leek

OVERVIEW

I have featured a few native alliums in this book. What's nice about the wild leek is that it does well in part shade. It also has delicate, white-green flowers versus the typical purple color of alliums. Each plant has two to three fleshy leaves at its base, about a foot long. They grow from the bulb and have a very strong onion flavor and aroma. The flower stalk is usually 6"-12" high and produces a small greenish-white cluster of flowers at the top. The showy cluster consists of small white to light green, six-petal flowers. The flowers also emit a strong onion odor.

GROWING NOTES

The wild leek is native to woods and forests. It does like a little more sun in the early spring when the leaf canopy in its native woodland is not as thick. This budding canopy creates a dappled shade versus deep shade. Like its home, it prefers humus-rich soil with plenty of compost and moisture. It can be propagated by seeds, although from my own experience, this can be difficult with alliums. Propagation is easiest by dividing the bulbs.

Zone: 4-8

Bloom time: Spring

DYK?

Native Americans ate wild leeks often and used them in soup

Native Regions

spring beauty
Claytonia virginica

aka: fairy spuds, wild potato

OVERVIEW

Like its name, this native plant is an early spring bloomer. It covers the ground with tiny flowers for two to three weeks. Each flower features five petals in either pink or white colors with dark pink veining. These sweet, dainty flowers remind me of charming "candy striper" volunteers at hospitals. Leaves are grass like and grow halfway up the plants. Various bees frequent it for its nectar as well as its pollen.

GROWING NOTES

This plant likes moisture as well as rich, loamy soil. It can't be propagated through tuber division, but the easier way is by seed. In fact, it's self-sows easily, so it can be aggressive and push out other plants nearby. Division or thinning every few years is prudent.

Zone: 3-9

Bloom time: late spring-early summer

DYK?

Pioneers, insects, and wildlife have been known to eat the tubers like potatoes

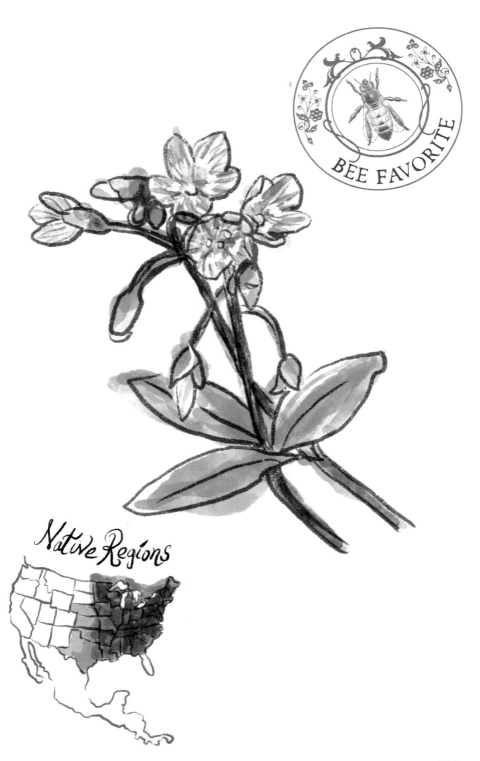

BEE FAVORITE

Native Regions

sharp-lobed hepatica

Hepatica acutiloba

aka: sharp-lobed liverwort, sharp-lobed liverleaf

OVERVIEW

This interesting perennial keeps its dark brown-green colored leaves throughout the winter. The leaves themselves give this plant it's other common names, on account of their shape. The leathery leaves are 2" long and 4" wide, and look like a piece of liver. It's one of the earliest spring wildflowers in the woods. Its cold hardiness is due to the leaves' coat of fine hairs which protect the plant from frost. The flowers themselves range from blue, pink or white. Each bloom has five to eighteen petals with abundant pistils and stamens. These produce copious amounts of pollen and nectar, making a veritable buffet for bees.

GROWING NOTES

This plant is natural to woodland environments. So it prefers light shade and calcium-rich soil with lots of natural compost and moisture. It does not like things too wet. This plant can tolerate drier, rockier gardens as long as it has consistent moisture. Propagation can be from seed or root division. Root division may be quicker, as long as you keep the transplants consistently moist until they're established. Seeds tend to take longer to germinate and flower.

Zone: 3-7

Bloom time: early spring

BEE FAVORITE

Native Regions

155

prairie shooting star

Dodecatheon meadia

aka: prairie pointers, cranesbill, rooster heads

OVERVIEW

One look at these unique native wildflowers, and you'll understand why they're called prairie shooting stars. The flower's petal clusters fall back and come together very much like the tail of a shooting star. The basal leaves grow in a circular clump at ground level and send thin stems up to carry the delicate blooms. The abundant blooms are usually six to forty per cluster. Flower colors range from white, pink, rose and fuchsia. Though the petals fall back toward the sky, the flowers themselves nod down. Sadly, this flower is becoming very rare to find in the wild, on account of aggressive collectors and pesticide drift. If you see it in the wild, take a picture and let it be.

GROWING NOTES

Prairie shooting stars are an open woodland native. Because of its native home, it prefers rich, loamy, moist soil with a slight acidity. It can tolerate slightly sunnier locations. But be careful to keep the moisture consistent during bloom time. Once the flowers fade it can cope with droughtier conditions. Propagation can be from root division, root cuttings, or seeds. However, propagating these plants from seed can be tricky. Starter plants are very fragile.

Zone: 4-8

Bloom time: mid spring

Native Regions

twin leaf

Jeffersonia diphylla

aka: Jeffersonia, rheumatism root

OVERVIEW

This plant almost looks like a pollinator itself. Its deep blue-green compound leaves mirror each other, looking like 6" long butterfly wings. These 'wings' sit atop long, thin stems, and look like they flutter in the breeze. The plant itself grows in thick clumps. When in bloom, it features showy little creamy-white flowers with eight small petals around a bright yellow center. The flowers, sadly, are short-lived and are very delicate. But the unique butterfly-winged leaves add an interesting green texture for the rest of the growing season. The plant was actually named after Thomas Jefferson from a contemporary of his. Unfortunately, this plant is becoming endangered in some states.

GROWING NOTES

A woodland native, it prefers soil like its forest home; moist, mulched and well drained. In fact, it does prefer consistent moisture. So in hotter weather, water is more important to keep the roots cool. Propagation by seed takes a long time. It takes a year for plants to flower, and young plants don't compete well with more aggressive plants in the area. Root division for propagation is quicker.

Zone: 5-7

Bloom time: mid spring

Native Regions

cream false indigo

Baptisia bracteata

aka: long bract wild indigo, plains wild indigo

OVERVIEW

This plant is part of the pea family, making it similar to lupine or other pea cousins. This plant grows to a shrub-like size. It becomes bushy with full, dense, cascading spikes of a dozen small, pea-like white or cream flowers. The flower clusters can also be light yellow. Velvety palm-shaped green leaves add to the plant's bushy appearance. Sadly, this plant is endangered in some states, and nurseries don't readily carry it. But it starts easily enough from seeds. So adding this to your yard is easy and can help bring the species back to safer levels.

GROWING NOTES

Cream false indigo prefers average to dry soil that's well-drained. It is a versatile grower, and can adapt to many locations including drier, sandier soils. Propagation is best by seed. In fact, it grows quickly and easily by seed.

Zone 4-9

Bloom time: early spring

Native Regions

wild columbine

Aquilegia canadensis

*aka: Eastern columbine, meeting houses,
red columbine*

OVERVIEW

This is one of my favorites plants to bring some color to shady areas. This plant has elegant, nodding 2" flowers, each with five scarlet petals that almost look like fingers or gloves. The blooms can range in color from salmon, pink or yellow but are usually scarlet red. Nectar fills the centers of these flowers that bees and hummingbirds love. Blooms last a long time making it a great nectar source for the pollinators. Once the blooms go to seed, the remaining foliage is delicate and frilly, adding a nice, green texture to a shadier garden.

GROWING NOTES

A very flexible woodlands plant, it can manage many soil conditions, even rocky slopes. It can grow in alkaline to moderately acidic soil and is very adept during dry spells. Wild columbine prefers part shade for plenty of blooms. But it can grow in shadier areas as well as sunnier areas, but both may affect the number of blooms. Wild Columbine is best propagated from seed. The rootstock is sometimes hard to divide with success.

Zone: 3-8

Bloom time: mid spring-early summer

BEE FAVORITE

Native Regions

wild blue phlox

Phlox divaricata

aka: wild sweet William, woodland phlox, blue phlox, Louisiana phlox, wild blue phlox, blue woodland phlox, wood phlox

OVERVIEW

What makes this woodland flowering native so unique is that it's one of very few blue colored flowering shade plants. This plant produces loose, flat clusters of flowers atop hairy, sticky stems. Each fragrant tubular flower is 1" across, with five petals. Wild blue phlox is predominantly found with blue blooms, but can also be found in pale blue lavender, deep violet, bright white, or even a rosy red. It's a fast-spreading plant if left alone. Its leafy shoots at its base spread along the ground, creating new roots along the way.

GROWING NOTES

Being a woodland native, wild blue phlox prefers loamy, moist soil with moderate acidity. It prefers part shade but can tolerate deeper shade. Unlike its other phlox cousins, propagation by seed is difficult, as these seeds are slow to germinate. Therefore, root division is best for quick propagation of this plant.

Zone: 3-8

Bloom time: mid spring-early summer

BUTTERFLY FAVORITE

Native Regions

Jacob's ladder

Polemonium reptans

aka: Greek valerian, creeping Jacob's ladder, sweet root, blue-eyed Susan

OVERVIEW

Similar to its name, Jacob's ladder produces ladder-like, pinnate, compound leaves in abundance along forest floors. These ladder-like leaves create large, frilly mounds. During its bloom time, loose flower clusters cling to the tops of its arched, thin stems. Each flower cluster is made up of light blue, bell-shaped flowers, each about ¾" long. This plant is another one of those rare occasions where you find light blue flowers as a woodland native that thrives in shadier spots. That makes these plants sought after by gardeners everywhere

GROWING NOTES

This is a woodland plant, so it is native to rich, moist woodlands as well as tree-lined streams. So it prefers cooler areas with partial shade. It can tolerate sunnier locations in cooler climates, as long as moisture is consistent. It is easily propagated by seeds and self-sows readily in optimal conditions.

Zone: 3-8

Bloom time: mid spring to early summer

Native Regions

groundnut

Apios americana

*aka: wild bean, Indian potato,
potato bean, hopniss*

OVERVIEW

This is one of the few climbing vines I've added to the book. The unique compact clusters of flowers actually look like flowering peas. Groundnut is part of the pea family. The clusters have a unique tan/red to purple/red color which grows on aggressive vines. This plant makes for good groundcover or can be trained on a gate or trellis. It's been a foraging crop for beans as well as for its roots, and a food source for early settlers. It's tuber roots, once cooked, has been used as food by the native Americans, and the cooked seeds can also be eaten. It's an aggressive grower, so if you need a wall or gate covered quickly, this is your plant. Once the plant goes to seed, the compact leaflets along the vines can be enjoyed throughout the growing season.

GROWING NOTES

As mentioned, this is a quick growing vine and very aggressive. It is also very flexible regarding soil conditions. It does like consistent moisture. It is best propagated by dividing the tubers.

Zone: 3-9

Bloom time: summer

Native Regions

purple trillium
Trillium erectum

aka: wake robin, stinking Benjamin, red trillium

OVERVIEW

Purple trilliums are one of the first natives I received as a gift. My friend who has advocated for natives for years (pretty much before it was trendy) gave me her splittings. This plant gives me some early spring color and growth year after year. The blooms in the spring feature three diamond-shaped leaves on each stem. And includes a three-petaled nodding flower, often in a striking crimson to maroon color. It does have a stinky odor that attracts its major pollinator, the green flesh fly. Its roots run very deep making it incredibly hearty and versatile.

GROWING NOTES

This flower is native to woodlands. So it likes loamy soil with a lot of leaves, debris, and compost. It prefers mulch and debris especially before winter, like its woodland habitat. It prefers moist soil and can tolerate shade as well as sun. Propagation is best by seed or root division.

Zone 2-8

Bloom time: spring

Native Regions

mayapple

Podophyllum peltatum

*aka: mandrake, American mandrake,
wild mandrake, duck's foot*

OVERVIEW

This is a distinct plant seen often on woodland walks. It makes for perfect
ground cover and spreads abundantly across forest floors. Plants include either
a nonflowering stem bearing a single broadleaf. This large leaf looks like an
umbrella, with five to nine lobes. Or the plant produces a flowering stem with
a pair of broad leaves that produce a flower between them. The flower drops
down between the two leaves, looking like it's nodding or napping. The
flowers are very aromatic and include six to nine waxy white petals. The flowers
produce fruit that looks like a small, green apple. This apple provides food for
woodland animals.

GROWING NOTES

This plant is native to woodland habitats. If you've seen it along the forest
floor, you can surmise that it's not choosy about soils. It can grow and self
propagate. Mayapples can tolerate deeper shade as well as part shade, adding to
its flexibility. Due to its native habitat, it prefers soil with consistent moisture.
It also likes a lot of mulch and leaves over the winter. Propagation is best by
dividing its rhizomes. Though people can get a rash from doing this procedure,
so use gloves. Mayapples can get aggressive once established, so be sure that
you're giving it plenty of space.

Zone: 3-8

Bloom time: mid spring to early summer

Native Regions

DYK?

Most parts of the May Apple are poisonous to people.

spiderwort
Tradescantia obiensis

OVERVIEW

Spiderwort gets its name because it was considered to be a treatment for spider bites. Enjoyed by gardeners for its color in shadier spots, the three-petaled blue flowers are sadly short-lived. They only bloom for about three weeks in the spring in colors that range from lavender to bright pink to white. I actually have some spiderwort in my garden that's yellow! The shadier the area, the droopier the plants, and they may fall over. More shade affects the amount and lifespan of the blooms, too. When plants flop over, the jointed stems will root if they hit the ground and then make a baby plant right there.

GROWING NOTES

Spiderwort prefers moist, well-drained soil. It can handle deeper shade but as mentioned, too much shade and the plants need to be staked. Propagation is easily done through stem cuttings, dividing up the roots or by seed. As mentioned above, it propagates itself readily by rooting at its joints.

Zone 4-9

Bloom time: late spring

DYK?

Spiderwort changes color when radiation is present, which is why you may see fields of it near nuclear power plants.

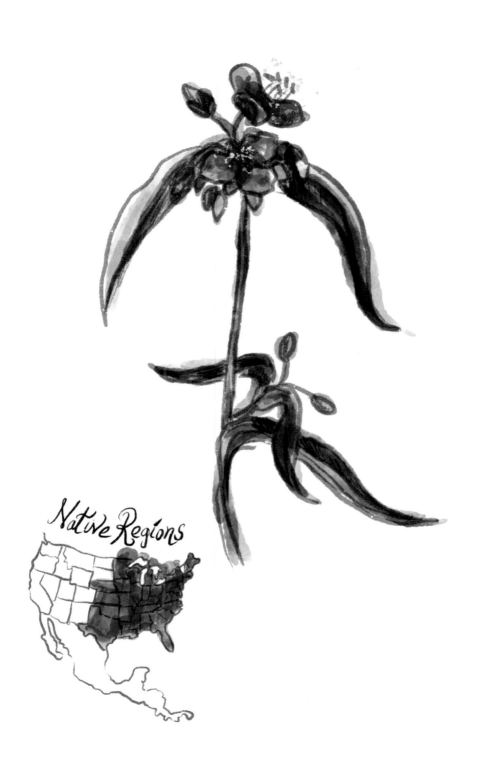

Native Regions

Canada anemone

Anemone canadensis

aka: windflower

OVERVIEW

This is one of the first flowers to bloom on the prairie and a favorite among bees who love to pollinate it. Because of its early bloom time, it's a great food source for bees early in the season who are getting started. The 1" to 2" flowers are a glimmering, white color with five petals around a bright yellow center. The single flowers sit on long stems and bear leaves that each have five to seven deep lobes. Its often referred to as a windflower, because its long stems flutter in the breeze, sending the seeds off to greener pastures.

GROWING NOTES

This is a plant from the open prairies, so it's not fussy about soil. It prefers moderate moisture and neutral acidity. If it's happy in a spot. it can get pretty aggressive and crowd out other plants. So dividing plants every few years is prudent. Especially because it self propagates by seed easily. Propagation can also be by rhizome division.

Zone: 2-6

Bloom time: mid-late spring

BEE FAVORITE

Native Regions

177

large blue flag

Iris versicolor

aka: wild iris, blue flag

OVERVIEW

Large blue flag is actually part of the iris family, but not to be confused with traditional irises. This native wildflower grows in wet habitats and moist areas, but the flower does look like a small iris. Leaves are firm and sword-shaped, about 8"-36" long. They surround a thick stalk supporting one to two iris-like flowers. Blue flag colors range from blue to purple. Mother Nature placed the colors on the iris in a way to help pollinators find the nectar. Each bloom has dark purple lines by the sepal, guiding the pollinator inward where the nectar is. While making its way inward, a pollinator pollinates the whole time. The blooms themselves have three true flower petals that point up and three petal-looking sepals that point down. It's these sepals that flutter in the breeze, looking like a flag, thus the name 'large blue flag'.

GROWING NOTES

As I mentioned before, this plant is native to wet habitats. So it is happier in wet, moist areas. But it is a flexible grower and can thrive in most garden environments. It's a very easy to care for plant, and can tolerate full sun too. It can be propagated by dividing the rhizomes, but care must be taken when doing this chore. Some people have reported sensitivity to the rhizomes and get rashes on their hands. Gardeners should wear gloves to be careful. Propagation can also be by seeds but it can take years.

Zone: 2-7

Bloom time: late spring-early summer

Native Regions

yellow lady's-slipper

Cypripedium parviflorum

aka: moccasin flower

OVERVIEW

This lovely woodland wildflower is rarely found in the wild, sadly because botanists and gardeners pull it up to save or transplant (please, don't!). It's a form of an orchid, which gives it a unique and exotic look when finding it in the forest. The bloom itself has a yellow pouch-shaped lower "lip", about 2" long, with a 'V' shape above the opening or "mouth". Around the opening of the bloom are red speckled markings, contrasting nicely with its golden-yellow color. Adding to its unique look are 3 to 6 leaves attached to the stem that 7" long that have deep veining, giving it a striped look. Each plant produces only one or two flowers. Some consider it to look like a slipper or shoe.

GROWING NOTES

As a woodland native, yellow lady slipper prefers shady, damp habitats with well-drained soil. This flower can actually tolerate full shade but does best with a little bit of sun. It can be propagated by seed or rhizome division.

Zone: 3-7

Bloom time: mid spring to early summer

Native Regions

PART
SHADE

wood lily

Lilium philadelphicum

aka: prairie lily, western red lily

OVERVIEW

I was fortunate to have inherited these flowers in our first home's garden and fell in love with them. There are very few lilies that can grow in shadier areas, and the wood lily is one of them. In fact, it is so sought after that they are now considered very rare, and on their way to being on the endangered species list. Unfortunately, people pluck the flowers when discovered in the woods. Its bulb never recovers, and the plant doesn't get a chance to self-propagate by seed without the flower. If you find them at a nursery, be sure to ask questions and make sure they are propagating them responsibly. The bright orange flowers make quite a statement, with six flower petals that point upward. The lilies range in color from a yellow-orange to a deep red-orange. They always feature purple spots, giving them an exotic look. The flowers appear on a stiff leaf-lined stalk, as a single flower or in clusters.

GROWING NOTES

As mentioned, these lilies like part shade, but can also tolerate full sun. They do need sun at least part of the day, so deep shade would not be ideal. This plant likes well-drained soil. Propagation is best by dividing bulbs once the plant has bloomed and died back. New bulbs grow around the mature bulb every year. So dividing is a bit necessary to keep blooms coming back and giving the plants enough room to flourish. Propagation can also be by seed, but it takes a bit longer.

Zone: 4-7

Bloom time: early to mid summer

Native Regions

TALL HEIGHT
24"–48" (2 feet–4 feet) High

turtlehead

Chelone glabra

aka: balmony, snakehead, fish mouth, shell flower, codhead, bitter herb

OVERVIEW

One look at these flowers and you understand why they're called "turtlehead". The 1" white flowers, often tinged with pink or yellow-green color, look like the open mouths of turtles. Flowers are found on top of the square, upright stems in compact, dense spikes. Flowers are accompanied by finely toothed, narrow green leaves. The blooms are pretty long lasting considering it's a flower that prefers partial shade. Besides their unique look, they're also sought after as a bee, butterfly and hummingbird magnet. Its flowers produce nectar that is very sweet, attracting many pollinators.

GROWING NOTES

Turtleheads are native to wetlands and pond shores. Therefore, they prefer very moist soil. But turtleheads can be flexible to regular garden conditions. They are not drought tolerant and do need consistent watering. This plant can tolerate full sun, too, as long as its consistently watered. They're typically an easy grower and not very fussy about the soil acidity either. Propagating turtleheads is easily done through root division, cuttings, or seeds.

Zone: 4-8

Bloom time: summer-early fall

BEE FAVORITE

BUTTERFLY FAVORITE

Native Regions

185

Great blue lobelia

Lobelia siphilitica

OVERVIEW

Great blue lobelia is known for its full, flowery spikes and sky blue flowers. Clusters sit on stalks that shoot up from a base of finely toothed, lance-shaped dark green leaves. Each small flower on the flower spike has two 'lips' above and three below. The lower rung has striping along the lower three pointing outward like a fan, making them very showy. Their copious amounts of nectar are what attracts many kinds of pollinators. Its long bloom time of two months also is a bonus.

GROWING NOTES

This plant doesn't mind some sunnier spots as long as it's in cooler climates. It prefers moist, well-drained, rich soil similar to its native wetter habitats. That being said, it can do well in normal garden conditions. But it won't do well in droughty, hot conditions and prefers consistent moisture. Propagation is best by root division and seeds. In fact, in optimal conditions, this plant will self sow readily.

Zone: 4-9

Bloom time: mid summer to early fall

Native Regions

cardinal flower

Lobelia cardinalis

OVERVIEW

This is a bright and loud wildflower. It gets its name from its bright red color, reminiscent of cardinal vestments. The flowers grow on 2-foot floral covered spikes, in deep red to scarlet red. Each flower is about 1" long and tubular, with three pointed lobes. Cardinal flower is a favorite of hummingbirds and pollinators because of its copious amounts of nectar. In fact, bumblebees have been known to chew through the base of the flowers, taking a short cut right to the nectar. The flowers sometime come in white or rose colors. They are accompanied by deep green, finely-toothed, lance-shaped 4" leaves. This tends to be a gardener's favorite because of the bright color it delivers so late in the growing season.

GROWING NOTES

Cardinal flowers are native to wetlands and swamps, so it prefers moist and very wet soil. However, it's very adaptable to normal garden conditions and very hardy. It can tolerate full sun. It does require moisture, so in full sun and hot days, it may need mulch and consistent water. It prefers to be mulched in colder zones, too, before winter. Propagation is easily achieved by seeds or root division.

Zone: 2-9

Bloom time: midsummer-early fall

BEE FAVORITE

BUTTERFLY FAVORITE

Native Regions

189

American bellflower

Campanula americana

aka: tall bellflower, American bluebell

OVERVIEW

Though it's called bellflower, the plant doesn't have bell-shaped flowers. Flat, five-pointed petal flowers, reminiscent of stars, scatter all up the stem of this plant. These 1" flowers are light blue with white centers. This native plant is another delayed germination flower, and bees love the pollen thus ensuring germination.

GROWING NOTES

American bellflower is not a fussy native plant but does like well-drained, moist soil. It does prefer a cold winter that signals the flowering cycle and ensures blooms in the summer. It does well in part shade areas but can handle sunnier locations. Propagation is best from seeds.

Zone: 3-8

Bloom time: summer

BEE FAVORITE

Native Regions

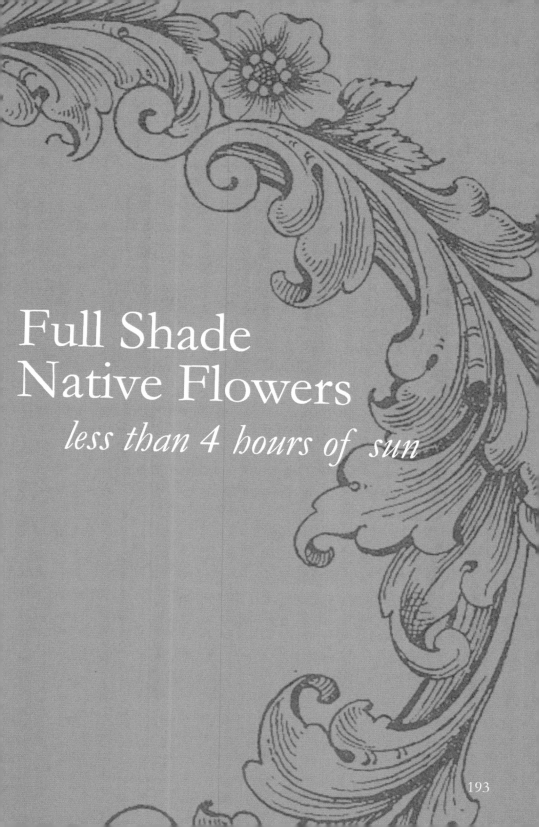

Full Shade
Native Flowers
less than 4 hours of sun

partridge berry

Mitchella repens

aka: twinberry, two-eyed berry, squaw berry, running fox

OVERVIEW

This native woodland plant likes to trail over the shady ground. It features dark green, glossy leaves that are evergreen and usually variegated. The rich, trailing foliage makes a lovely ground cover for shade gardens. The plant produces flowers that look like small trumpets in late spring. The blooms grow in pairs, usually white with a touch of light pink in color and are very fragrant. The flowers turn into berries, providing an important food source to woodland animals.

GROWING NOTES

Native to forests, it prefers cool, moist and shaded areas. It is very flexible with soil acidity. It prefers mulch, like its forest home. It can tolerate partial sun and some drought conditions. It tends to not be as aggressive a grower as other woodland ground covers. Propagation is best by dividing or cutting the runners and transplanting them. You can propagate this plant by seed, but the growing process is slower.

Zone: 4-9

Bloom time: late spring

Native Regions

bloodroot

Sanguinaria canadensis

OVERVIEW

This is another early blooming native plant, heralding spring. As its name suggests, the juice released by this plant's rhizomes, roots and stems is a blood-red color. It can stain your hands if you are not careful when planting or dividing it. The plant blooms in early to mid spring with 2" flowers that sit atop 8-16" stems. The flowers are similar to poppies, each with 8 to 12 white petals and bright yellow centers. The flowers themselves are short-lived.

After the flowers go to seed, the plant itself continues to stay green and grow. It boasts very attractive, deeply cut uniquely-shaped leaves. Greenery stays lush well into the early fall. Many gardeners plant bloodroot as much for the texture of the leaves as for the blooms. Short-lived as they are, the early flowers this plant produces give pollinators much-needed food early in the season.

GROWING NOTES

This plant is great for ground cover and is very flexible with its growing environment. It does need moist, well-drained soil-being a woodland plant. If the area is not well-drained, moisture will rot the rhizomes. In optimal growing conditions, it can get aggressive, crowding out other plants. Propagation is best through rhizome division or with seeds. In fact, if you keep the base of the plant clear from leaves and debris, the plant will self-sow. A word of caution, in colder zones, such as zones five on up, you may need to mulch this plant for the winter.

Zone: 3-8

Bloom time: early to mid spring

Native Regions

DYK?

The fluid from the plant's rhizomes and stems are toxic if ingested internally, but does have antiseptic properties.

wild ginger
Asarum canadensis

OVERVIEW

This native plant is called wild ginger because its edible roots taste like ginger. This plant makes great groundcover because the leaves stay green all summer long. The foliage gives your shadier gardens some nice texture and shape. The heart-shaped leaves grow right from the root system making it stemless. The leaves are broad, velvety and very unique. The whole plant, especially when it blooms, looks like something from an alien planet. Its exotic look is due to its flower bud. It lacks petals but is shaped like a small bell with flared pointed lobes the color of a deep purple-brown. Each plant only grows one flower, low to the ground and horizontally. This arrangement makes it very accessible for flesh flies and beetles to crawl into and pollinate.

GROWING NOTES

Native to woodlands, it prefers woodland-like environments. So it prefers consistent moisture. This plant can tolerate partial shade and slightly acidic soils. It can be propagated from seed but it's quite difficult. It's better to divide the rhizomes and transplanting those.

Zone 3-7

Bloom time: early-mid spring

Native Regions

foam flower

Tiarella cordifolia

aka: false miterwort

OVERVIEW

Like its name, its white flowers look frothy and foamy, like the top of a latte. The 8" to 12" spikes of flowers arise from a mound of heart-shaped leaves at the base. Tiny little petaled flowers that look like small tiaras (thus the Latin name "tiarella") fill the flowering spikes. The blooms are white with some light pink tones. I'm anxious to plant these in a very tough area under a very large bush. It gets shady and dry under this large shrub, making it difficult to plant any flowering plants. Foam flower should be able to thrive under this bush, where the only luck I've had to date are ferns.

GROWING NOTES

Foam flower is native to the woods, so it likes woodland conditions. Areas that have shade, moisture, and cool soil are ideal. It can tolerate part shade to deeper shade. It is easily grown in shady gardens and is propagated by dividing the roots as well as by seed.

Zone: 3-8

Bloom time: mid spring

Native Regions

yellow clintonia

Clintonia borealis

aka: corn lily, blue bead lily, dogberry, straw lily

OVERVIEW

This woodland flowering plant makes for wonderful ground cover for your shade beds. Yellow clintonia has a distinct flower, a distinct fruit, and distinct leaves. The two to four basal oval-shaped leaves are 6" long, and stay green well into the fall. This gives your garden and nice green texture throughout the growing season. The nodding bell-shaped lily flowers sit atop a 15-inch stem, usually one to eight flowers per cluster. The flowers are yellow to yellow-green in color and result in a blue colored fruit in the summer. It's this "Willie Wonka" looking fruit that gives it one of its common names, 'blue bead lily'.

GROWING NOTES

Yellow clintonia prefers cool, moist, acidic soil. It can tolerate part shade. And it prefers mulch in the fall in preparation for the winter months, a process like its native woodland habitat. Propagation of this flower is easiest by seed.

Zone: 2-7

Bloom time: mid spring-early summer

Native Regions

203

celandine poppy

Stylophorum diphyllum

aka: wood poppy

OVERVIEW

This woodland native is unique in that though it has a focused bloom time, it will flower periodically all throughout the growing season. This gives you little bursts of color throughout the summer in a part shade garden. Similar to its name, the flowers do look like poppies with its four petals in a bright, sunny yellow-orange color. The deep blue-green leaves look like oak trees and are deeply lobed. This pant is becoming rare to woodland habitats and endangered in Canada.

GROWING NOTES

Like most woodland natives, this plant prefers loamy, well-drained, moist soil. This flower tolerates part sun but prefers shade. Propagation by seed is very easy and self sows readily in its native habitat when it gets a chance too. Propagation can also be through rhizome division of smaller flower clumps.

Zone: 4-9

Bloom time: mid spring-early summer

wild bleeding-heart

Dicentra eximia

aka: fern leaf bleeding heart, fringed bleeding heart, turkey corn

OVERVIEW

This plant is in the same family as Dutchman's breeches, and you can see the relation when you look at the blooms. Flowers are heart-shaped, and usually light pink, lavender-pink to fuchsia. Each bloom is usually 1" and dangle from the long arching stems. Once the flowers fade, the plant's interesting fern-like leaves steal the show. They make a frilly mound at the plant's base, making the plant 12" to 30" wide. The flowers bloom all summer, unlike hybrid bleeding hearts. That makes it a plant they can add a lot of long-lasting colors in your shade garden.

GROWING NOTES

Wild bleeding heart does prefer shade and can tolerate part shade. If this plant gets too much sun, the leaves yellow and blooms wither. Native to woodland habitats, it prefers moist, humus-rich soil that's well-drained. Propagation is best by seed and self-sows but can be propagated by rhizome division. In fact, it is good to divide these plants occasionally to keep them healthy and blooming.

Zone: 3-9

Bloom time: summer

Native Regions

Virginia bluebells

Mertensia virginica

OVERVIEW

True to its name, this plant boasts delicate clusters of nodding blue, bell looking flowers. Each trumpet flower is 1" in length. These clusters dangle atop 18" long smooth stems. These sweet blooms don't start out as the delicate blue that they're known for. The buds actually present themselves as bright pink. Sometimes Virginia bluebells will present themselves in white or pink colors, too. Complementing these spring blooms are smooth-edged, bright green, 4" long oval leaves. They alternate up the stem. These unique, purple-blue happy flowers, appearing in early spring, is a welcome sight to tired winter eyes.

GROWING NOTES

This plant is native to moist woodlands but is very flexible to normal garden conditions. In fact, I have a few of them in my own part-shade garden bed. Like most woodland habitats, it does like rich, loamy, moist soil. It can't thrive in part sun, but the more sun it receives the more water it will need. Once the plant cycle is over, leaves will die to the ground and the plant will go dormant by midsummer. So when garden planning, make sure you surround bluebells with other late-blooming plants to disguise the bare area. Propagation can be through the division of the rhizomes or by seeds. In fact, it self-sows readily.

Zone: 3-8

Bloom time: early to mid spring

Native Regions

white wood aster

Eurybia divaricata; formerly Aster divaricatus

aka: white heart-leaved aster, white star aster,
wood aster

OVERVIEW

This aster is a favorite of mine. I always have trouble finding long-blooming plants for my shade garden. Wood aster not only gives you bright, fluffy white flowers earlier than other asters, but it is also a pollinator magnet. It is also a host plant to the Pearl Crescent Butterfly. This wildflower grows in loose clumps with effervescent, flat-topped flower clusters. The clusters are filled with small, starry 1" flowers. These clusters sit atop dark, wiry stems that have a slight zig-zag growth pattern. Each flower is composed of 9-10 circular ray petals around a yellow disc. The yellow centers turn into a mauve-purple center as the flowers mature, giving you extra interest in the garden. Adding some texture is its glossy deep green foliage. Its leaves are heart-shaped with toothy edges, about 3-6" long. These long bloomers can brighten up any shady garden-especially tough, dry areas. This unique plant is becoming rare to find and considered endangered in some areas. Plant it readily in your shade beds and see the pollinator traffic increase.

GROWING NOTES

Wood aster is native to dry, open woods, which gives you an indication of its hardiness. It is a very versatile grower and can tolerate dry, rocky soils to medium, moist soils. Thought it is a perfect shade plant, it can tolerate sunnier spots. It can thrive where many plants cannot-dry shady spots like under large trees and shady shrubs. It does need good circulation to prevent powdery mildew, so don't over-crowd it. This woodland flower can reseed itself readily and spreads also through its rhizomes. Propagation is best through root division.

Zone: 4-9

Bloom time: July-October

* For an aster that likes part shade but has a bigger native footprint in the midwest, try blue wood aster (Aster cordifolius). Flowers have a lavender-blue color.

BEE FAVORITE

Native Regions

BUTTERFLY FAVORITE

Solomon's seal

Polygonatum biflorum

OVERVIEW

If you're looking for something interesting for a shady area in your yard, look no further than Solomon's seal. The plant grows with thin, graceful arching stems that include two rows of 3"-5" leaves. Yellow-green flowers hang down along the arching stems like small, closed bells. The flowers themselves are 1" long, tubular and fragrant. The plant itself looks like if you were to shake it you would hear tingling bells ringing from the flowers. As in most shade plants, flowers don't last that long. So it's important to include shade plants with interesting texture and greenery throughout the season. Solomon's seal fits the bill. The plant can be found with simple green leaves or with attractive variegated leaves with white edging. The leaves stay green and grow all summer long, adding wonderful leafy arches to a back border or shady corner.

GROWING NOTES

This plant appears naturally in woodland habitats, therefore it prefers shady, moist soil. It can tolerate part shade, but consistent moisture is key. Propagation is best to through rhizome division or seeds.

Zone: 5-7

Bloom time: mid to late spring

Native Regions

Jack in the pulpit

Arisacma triphyllum

aka: Indian turnip, bog onion, brown dragon

OVERVIEW

This is a very unique, hooded bloom that is reminiscent of something from the dinosaur age. The distinctive bloom looks like a vase, sitting proudly on its own separate stalk. The blooms range in color from a vibrant green with a maroon or purple stripe, to a deep maroon-purple color with white stripes. Flanking these interesting plants are one to two large glossy leaves, divided into three leaflets. This plant blooms in its native woodland habitat from spring to early summer. It creates red berries in the fall, feeding many animals before the winter. This process, in turn, spreads seeds throughout the forest, allowing it to easily self-propagate.

GROWING NOTES

Being native to woodlands, it likes moist, well-drained soil with rich humus and leafy mulch. It is pretty flexible and easy to grow in regular garden soil. It does like shade and can handle some part sun. This plant spreads readily by seeds, though the germination process takes long. Propagation is quicker through root division.

Zone: 4-8

Bloom time: early spring-early summer

DYK?

It's called Jack in the pulpit because its upright "spadix" (flowery, fleshy spike), knows a "Jack". Jack looks like he is in his pulpit, preaching to his flock.

Native Regions

215

false Solomon's seal

Smilacina racemosa

*aka: Solomon's zigzag, Solomon's plume,
starry Solomon's plume*

OVERVIEW

Similar to Solomon seal, this plant has five to twelve leaves in two rows along its stem. But the leaves grow in a slight zig-zag to each other and have wavier edges. Where this plant differs from Solomon's seal is in the flowers. The clusters of 6"-12" plumes consist of frilly little $1/4$" creamy-white flowers, each with six small petals. The clusters sit at the end of thin, arching stems. They give the plant a look of small bottle brushes growing in the woods.

GROWING NOTES

This woodland plant flourishes in shade. But it can tolerate part shade as well as more sun. But the more sun this plant receives, the more stunted its growth and blooms. It prefers moist, well-drained, acidic soil. Propagation is best through rhizome division or seeds. Seeds, however, are slow to germinate.

Zone: 2-8

Bloom time: late spring

Native Regions

Bibliography

Why Native Plants Matter, National Audubon Society, https://www.audubon.org/content/why-native-plants-matter, May 20, 2019

Pollinators in Trouble, National Park Service, https://www.nps.gov/subjects/pollinators/pollinators-in-trouble.htm , May 11, 2019

Pollinators in Trouble Worldwide, Living on Earth, https://www.loe.org/shows/segments.html?programID=16-P13-00010&segmentID=4, May 20, 2019

Top Ten Native Plants to Attract Bees, Grow Native! Missouri Prairie Foundation, http://grownative.org/wp-content/uploads/2016/12/Top10GN_Dec_2016_AttractBees_Print.pdf, April 15, 2019

Heather McCargo, *IN THE SHADE: Gardening with Native Plants from the Woodland Understory*, Wild Seed Project, https://wildseedproject.net/2016/03/in-the-shade-gardening-with-native-plants-from-the-woodland-understory/February 10, 2019

Susan Reel, *Attracting Pollinators to Your Garden Using Native Plants,* Lola National Forest, https://www.fs.fed.us/wildflowers/pollinators/documents/AttractingPollinatorsV5.pdf, February 10, 2019

9 Types Bracts and Bracteoles | Plants, Biology Discussion, http://www.biologydiscussion.com/plants/bracts/9-types-bracts-and-bracteoles-plants/13339, April 15, 2019

Diagrams showing parts of a plant and a flower, http://www.saps.org.uk/secondary/teaching resources/707-parts-of-a-plant-and-a-flower, May 11, 2019

Lady Bird Johnson Garden Center, https://www.wildflower.org/plants/

United States Dept. of Agriculture, https://www.usda.gov/

http://www.missouribotanicalgarden.org/

Kirsten Sweet, *Gardening for Birds, Butterflies and Bees*, 2016, New York, NY, The Readers Digest Association, Inc.

Carolyn Harstad, *Go Native! Gardening with Native Plants,* 1999, Bloomington, IN, Indiana University Press

Janet Marinelli, *Going Native Biodiversity in our Own Backyard,* 1994, Brooklyn, NY, Brooklyn Botanic Garden Publications

Henry W. Art, *The Wildflower Gardener's Guide: Northeast, Mid-Atlantic, Great Lakes, and Eastern Canada Edition*, 1987, Garden Way Pub Co.

Henry W. Art, *The Wildflower Gardener's Guide: Midwest, Great Plains, and Canadian Prairies Edition, 1991,* Garden Way Pub Co.

Native Plant Retailers

I urge you to research your own local nature centers, community gardens and forest preserves for local plant sales. Many post these events on Facebook and on their sites. These sales can be a great way to buy rare natives inexpensively, and the funds usually support the sellers' respective missions.

The following is a list of nurseries selling natives by state. This list is not "canon". Stores open and close. More nurseries hop on the "native train" monthly as demand grows. Please scour your local area for nurseries to support. And perhaps ask your local nursery to start carrying natives. Sometimes all it takes is one loyal customer to make a change.

Online Retailers:

https://naturalcommunities.net

https://www.prairienursery.com

https://www.americanmeadows.com

https://www.opnseed.com

https://sunlightgardens.com

Nurseries by State: *(adapted from themeadowproject.org)*

MINNESOTA

Booming Native Plants, 2323 Co. Rd. 6, Barnum, MN 55707

Busse Gardens, 17160 245th Ave., Big Lake, MN 55309

Carlson Prairie Seed Farm, Inc., 2077 360th Ave., Lake Bronson

Ecoscapes Native Nursery, 721 Ladybird Lane, Burnsville, MN 55122

Itasca Ladyslipper Farm, 14958 River Road, Grand Rapids, MN 55744

Kaste Seed, Inc., 11779 410th Street SE, Fertile, MN 56540

Landscape Alternatives, Inc., 25316 St. Croix Trail, Shafer, MN 55074

Mark E. Gullickson, 10990 423rd St. SE, Fertile, MN 56540-9272

Minnesota State Forest Nurseries, Minnesota Dept. of Natural Resources, P.O. Box 95, Willow River, MN 55795

Mohn Seed Co., Rt. 1, Box 152, Cottonwood, MN 56229

Morning Sky Greenery, 44804 East Highway 28, Morris, MN 56267

Minnesota Native Landscapes, 8740 77th St NE, Otsego, MN 55362

Natural Shore Technologies, Inc, 6275 Pagenkopf Rd, Maple Plain, MN 55359

Norfarm Seeds, Inc., P.O. Box 725, 104 Minnesota Ave., Bemidji, MN 56619

North American Prairies Company, 11754 Jarvis Ave., Annadale, MN 56379

Northern Lights Silviculture, 41481 County Road 63, Cohasset, MN 55721

Out Back Nursery, Inc., 15280 110th St. S., Hastings, MN 55033

Prairie Hill Wildflowers, 8955 Lemond Rd. Ellendale, MN 56026

Prairie Moon Nursery, 31837 Bur Oak Ln, Winona, MN 55987-9515

Prairie Restorations, Inc., P.O. Box 327, Princeton, MN 55371

Red Lake Forestry Greenhouse, P.O. Box 643, Red Lake Band of Chippewa Indians, Redby, MN 56670

Shooting Star Native Seeds, 20740 County Road 33, Spring Grove, MN 55974

Spangle Creek Labs/Itasca Ladyslipper Farm, William or Carol Steele, 21950 County Rd. 445, Bovey, MN 55709-9547

Wildlife Habitat Seed Co., 5114 NE 46th St., Owatonna, MN 55060

WISONSIN:

Agrecol Corp., 2918 Agriculture Dr., Madison, WI 53718

Bluestem Farm, S5920 Lehman Rd., Baraboo, WI 53913

Everwilde Farms, Inc., PO Box 40, Sand Creek, WI 54765

Hayward State Forest Nursery, Wisconsin Dept. of Natural Resources, 16133 W. Nursery Road, Hayward, WI 54843

Hild & Associates, 326 Glover Rd., S. River Falls, WI 54022 Orders: 800/790-9495

J & J Transplant Aquatic Nursery Inc., W4980 County Rd. W., P.O. Box 227, Wild Rose, WI 54984-0227

Kester's Wild Game Food Nurseries, Inc., P.O. Box 516, Omro, WI 54963

Order: 800/558-8815

Kettle Moraine Natural Landscaping, W996 Birchwood Dr., Campbellsport, WI 53010

Marshland Transplant Aquatic Nursery, P.O. Box 1, Berlin, WI 54923

Patty's Plants Natural and Organic Garden Supply, 220 S. Janesville St., Milton, WI 53563

Prairie Ridge Nursery, 9738 Overland Rd., Mt. Horeb, WI 53572-2832

Reeseville Ridge Nursery, 512 S. Main St., P.O. Box 171, Reeseville, WI 53579

Stone Silo Prairie Gardens, 4500 Oak Ridge Circle, DePere, WI 54115

Taylor Creek Restoration Nurseries, 17921 W Smith Rd., P.O. Box 256, Brodhead, WI 53520

Wildlife Nurseries, Inc., P.O. Box 2724, Oshkosh, WI 54903

Wilson State Forest Nursery , 5350 Highway 133 East, P.O. Box 305, Boscobel, WI 53808

Woods' Edge Farm, 532 Stanek Rd., Muscoda, WI 53573

ILLINOIS:

Aquatic Nursery, 38W135 McDonald Rd., Elgin, IL

Blazing Star Nursery, 2107 Edgewood Drive, Woodstock, IL 60098

City Grange, 5500 N Western Ave, Chicago, IL 60625

Christy Webber Farm & Garden, 2833 W Chicago Ave, Chicago, IL 60612

Earthwild Gardens, 1479 Potawatomi Road, Grayslake, IL 60030

Earthskin Nursery , 9331 NCR 3800E, Mason City, IL 62664

Farmer's Market Garden Center, 4110 N Elston Ave, Chicago, IL 60618

Glacier Oaks Nursery, 8216 White Oaks Rd, Harvard, IL 60033

Lee's Gardens, 25986 Sauder Rd, Tremont, IL 61568

Mason State Nursery IL Dept. of Natural Resources, Forest Resources, 17855 N. Country Road, 2400 E. Topeka, IL 61567

Natural Garden Natives™ sold by Midwest Groundcovers LLC, P.O. Box 748 , St. Charles, IL 60174

Possibility Place Nursery, 7548 W. Monee-Manhattan Road, Monee, IL 60449

Prairie Earth Nursery, Jim Alwill, Rural Route 1 Box 151, Bradford, IL 61421

Simply Native Nursery, 681 State Hwy 135, Alexis, IL 61412

St. Aubin Nursery, Todd Sullivan, 35445 Irene Road, Kirkland, IL 60146

Union State Tree Nursery, IL Dept. of Conservation Forest Resources, 3240 State Forest Rd., Jonesboro, IL 62952

Wilson Seed Farms, Chris Wilson, 10872 1400 E. Street, Tiskilwa, IL 61368

INDIANA:

Earthly Goods, Ltd., P.O. Box 614, 620 E. Main St, New Albany, IN 47150

Indiana Division of Forestry, 15508 W. 700 N, Medaryville, IN 47957

The Land Nursery, 513 Sharon Rd., West Lafayette, IN 47906

Munchkin Nursery and Gardens LLC, 323 Woodside Dr. N.W., Depauw, IN 47115-9039

Vallonia State Nursery, 2782 W. Co. Rd. 540 S., P.O. Box 218, Vallonia, IN 47281

Winterhaven Wildflowers & Native Plant Preserve, 5724 S 900 W, West Point, IN

Cardno Native Plant Nursery, 128 Sunset Drive, Walkerton, IN 46574

Heartland Restoration Services, Inc., 14921 Hand Road, Fort Wayne, IN 46818

Hensler Nursery, Inc., 5715 North 750 E., P.O. Box 58, Hamlet, IN 46532

Spence Restoration Nursery, Inc., Kevin Tungesvick, 2220 E. Fuson Rd., Muncie, IN 47302

Woody Warehouse, Inc., Pete Berg, P.O. Box 259/ 3216 W. 850 N., Lizton, IN 46149

IOWA:

Allendan Seed, 1966 175th Lane, Winterset, IA 50273

Diversity Farms, 25494 320th, Dedham, IA 51440

Iawisil Forest Nursery, 1621 McCabe Lane, Cascade, IA 52033

Ion Exchange, 1878 Old Mission Dr., Harpers Ferry, IA 52146-7533

Kingfisher Farms, 29633 170th Ave., Long Grove, IA 52756

McGinnis Tree and Seed Company, 309 E. Florence, Glenwood, IA 51534

Osenbaugh's Grass Seeds, 11009 542nd St., Lucas, IA 50151

Reeves Wildflower Nursery, 28431 200th St., Harper, IA 52231

State Forest Nursery, Iowa Department of Natural Resources, 2404 South Duff Avenue, Ames, IA 50010

KANSAS:

De Lange Seed, Inc., P.O. Box 7, Girard, KS 66743

Kansas Forest Service, 2610 Claflin Rd., Manhattan, KS 66502-1798

Kaw River Restoration Nurseries, 1269 N. 222nd Rd., Baldwin City, KS 66006

Sharp Bros. Seed Co., 1005 S. Sycamore, Healy, KS 67850

Sunflower Farms, 1065 S. Olive St., Cherryvale, KS 67335

Vinland Valley Nursery, 1606 N. 600 Rd., Baldwin City, KS 66006

NEBRASKA:

PE Allen Farm Supply, 89400 497th Ave, Bristow, NE 68719.

Prairie Legacy, Kay Kottas, 1225 Co Rd U, Western, NE 68464.

Stock Seed Farms, Rod Fritz, 28008 Mill Rd., Murdock, NE 68407-2350.

NORTH DAKOTA:

Towner State Nursery, 878 Nursery Rd., Towner, ND 58788-9500

OHIO:

B.C. Nursery, 4183 S.R. 276, Batavia, OH 45103

Companion Plants, Inc., 7247 N. Coolville Ridge Rd., Athens, OH 45701.

Envirotech Consultants/ Nursery, 5380 Township, 143 NE, Somerset, OH 43783

Freshwater Farms of Ohio, Inc., 2624 North US Hwy. 68, Urbana, OH 43078

Keystone Flora, LLC Native Plants Nursery of Southwest Ohio, P.O. Box 20109, Cincinnati, Ohio 45220

Land Reforms Greenhouse, 35703 Loop Rd., Rutland, OH 45775

Mary's Plant Farm, 2410 Lanes Mill Rd., Hamilton, OH 45013.

Ohio Prairie Nursery, PO Box 174, Hiram, Ohio 44234

Scioto Gardens, 3351 State Route 37 W., Delaware, OH 43015

MICHIGAN:

Cold Stream Farm, 2030 Free Soil Rd., Free Soil, MI 49411

Hartmann's Plant Company, Lacota Native Plants, P.O Box 100, Lacota, MI 49063-0100

Hidden Savanna Nursery, 18 N Van Kal Street, Kalamazoo, MI 49009

J.W. Toumey Nursery, P.O. Box 340, Watersmeet, MI 49969

Lodi Farms Nursery, 2880 South Wagner Road, Ann Arbor, MI 48103

Michigan Wildflower Farm, 11770 Cutler Rd., Portland, MI 48875

Native Connections, 17080 Hoshel Rd., Three Rivers, MI 49093

The Native Plant Nursery, Inc, P.O. Box 7841, Ann Arbor, MI 48107

Newaygo Conservation District Nursery, 1725 E. 72nd St., Newaygo, MI 49337

Oakland Wildflower Farm, LLC, 520 North Hurd Road, Ortonville, MI 48462

Oikos Tree Crops, P.O. Box 19425, Kalamazoo, MI 49019-0425

Sandhill Farm, 11250 10 Mile Road, Rockford, MI 49341

Wetlands Nursery, 13428 Caberfae Hwy , Wellston, MI 49689

WILDTYPE Design, Native Plants & Seed, 900 North Every Rd., Mason, MI 48854

MISSOURI:

Bowood Farms, Lizzy Rickard, 4605 Olive St, St. Louis, MO 63108

Elixir Farm Botanicals, LLC, County Rd. 158, Brixey, MO 65618

George O. White State Forest Nursery, 14027 Schafer Rd., Licking, MO 65542

Hamilton Native Outpost, 16786 Brown Rd., Elk Creek, MO 65464

Missouri Wildflowers Nursery, 9814 Pleasant Hill Rd., Jefferson City, MO 65109-9805

Osage Prairie Mercantile, P.O. Box 152, Clinton, MO 64735

SOUTH DAKOTA:

Wilber's Seed Solutions, 800 N Broadway, P.O. Box 41, Miller, SD 57362

Learn more about Native Plants at some of these Online Resources:

https://wildones.org

https://www.minnesotawildflowers

https://grownative.org

https://themeadowproject.com
Click on a state to find native plant nurseries near you.

https://www.fs.fed.us

https://indiananativeplants.org

http://www.plantnative.org

http://www.heinzetrust.org

https://www.audubon.org

https://www.indianawildlife.org

https://www.wildflower.org

https://www.nwf.org

https://garden.org

https://choosenatives.org

Flower Parts 101

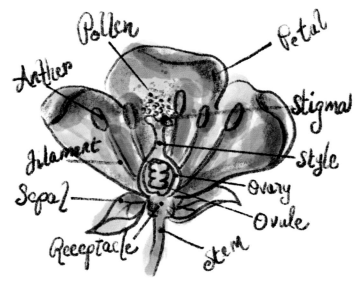

Pollen • Petal • Anther • Stigma • Filament • Style • Sepal • Ovary • Ovule • Receptacle • Stem

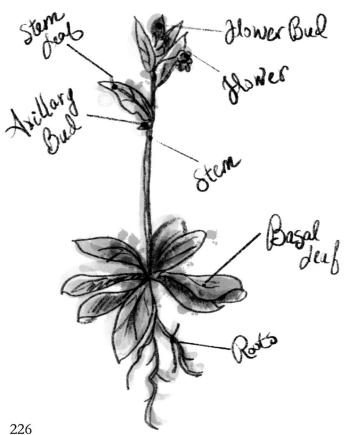

Stem leaf • Flower Bud • Flower • Axillary Bud • Stem • Basal leaf • Roots

Bract

Flower

Bract

Flower

Flower Cluster

Bracts

Bracts

A note about bracts:

Not to make this a big botany lesson, but you may have seen the word "bracts" in some of my descriptions. A bract looks often like a flower petal and part of the flower but is actually a modified, specialized leaf. They can play many roles, depending on the flower. They can be there for the protection of the buds, to attract pollinators, attract and catch insects or provide nutrition. Whereas the flower consists only of 4 parts; sepals, petals, stamens, and pistils. Bracts, being none of these, are pretty much the flower's "wingman".

ABOUT ME:

I grew up around food and gardening. My family inducted me into what I call the "Taylor Street Italian Cooks Club," from the moment I could hold a wooden spoon to stir tomato sauce. My Nonno started my love of gardening by taking me to their apartment roof. There, we cared for countless tomato plants growing in rusty tin cans. As I grew older, I expanded those passions to other creative outlets like garden design, crafting and writing. But art was always at my core. I followed it to a degree in Advertising Art from Columbia College Chicago, with an emphasis in illustration. With a degree in hand, I began a long career in the creative field of advertising. My love of food helped me excel and grow a large variety of food brands. This list includes Kraft Foods, Kellogg's, Quaker Oats, Smithfield Foods, Whole Foods Market, and many others. The more I learned, about food, the more I loved it, and the more I learned about preparing it.

As the marketing landscape has evolved, so have my interests and skills. Nothing has changed it faster than social media. I started a food & lifestyle blog in 2008 called the urbandomesticdiva.com. For over ten years I've shared recipes, cooking tips, craft ideas, and gardening how-tos. It is now a well-attended community with a love of sharing ways to make our world lovelier, tastier and more creative. It has evolved to include a gift shop featuring my hand-designed products.

My experience with food garnered a membership into the Chicago chapter of Les Dames D'Escoffier. This is a female-led, worldwide philanthropic society. It consists of professional women leaders in the fields of food, fine beverage, and hospitality. I have served on the board for 2 years. I continue to help with all the events and activities as our chapter's resident art director.

With all my "downtime" I'm a very involved mom of a teen and a cat. I'm in 2 book clubs. I fly-fish with my husband. And I run a freelance business with clients such as The French Pastry School, Quaker Oats Company, and the American Dairy Association. Between all this, I try to find time to snuggle with my husband while watching reruns of Britcoms.

You can stay up on all the crazy, as well as yummy content, at the following cyber spots. I look forward to hearing from you!

urbandomesticdiva.com	_etsy.com_	Marketing?
Facebook	_urbandomesticdivashop.com_	_LinkedIn_
Twitter		_Floracaputo.com_
YouTube		
Pinterest		

Notes

Notes

Notes

Notes

Notes

Index

The hum of
bees is the
voice of
the garden.
~Elizabeth Lawrence